YOU
Can Preach
to the Kids,
TOO!

YOU
Can Preach to the Kids,
TOO!

Designing Sermons for Adults *and* Children

Carolyn C. Brown

Abingdon Press
Nashville

YOU CAN PREACH TO THE KIDS, *TOO!*

Library of Congress Cataloging-in-Publication Data

Brown, Carolyn C. (Carolyn Carter), 1947-
   You can preach to the kids, too! : designing sermons for adults and children / Carolyn C. Brown.
     p.   cm.
   ISBN 0-687-06157-1 (alk. paper)
   1. Preaching to children.   I. Title.
BV4235.C4B76   1997
251′.53—dc21
                                                            97-26777
                                                            CIP

99 00 01 02 03 04 05 06 — 10 9 8 7 6 5 4 3 2

MANUFACTURED IN THE UNITED STATES OF AMERICA

Contents

Introduction

YOU **can preach to the kids, too!**

Yes, you! Preaching to kids does not require some super skills or deep-seated personality traits that you either have or do not have. Just as anyone who is willing to undertake the discipline can preach to adults, anyone who is willing to undertake some disciplines on behalf of the children in the congregation can preach to the kids.

You CAN preach to the kids, too!

Anyone who is willing can preach to children IF you have mastered a few skills. This book identifies the skills, suggests ways to develop them, and offers resources. It is a do-it-yourself preaching seminar offering a few new insights and skills with which to enrich your preaching.

You can PREACH to the kids, too!

For most adults the sermon is the heart of Sunday worship. But when worship planners try to include children in Sunday worship, we generally focus on the liturgy. We assume that if we can draw children into the songs and prayers of the congregation, we have fulfilled our responsibility to them. We can, then, focus on the adults during the sermon. When we do this, we shortchange the children. Children face daily situations that are as challenging as those that are faced by adults. They need to hear about God's love and forgiveness, and think with the rest of the congregation about what it means to be among God's people. We have a responsibility to preach to the kids, as well as sing and pray with them.

You can preach TO THE KIDS, too!

We assume that kids do not—even cannot—listen to sermons. In spite of all the wiggles and complaints, children repeatedly disprove this assumption by their often startling comments. They do listen to sermons—or at least to parts of sermons. When the preacher and the children's parents encourage them, they listen even more. This book offers specific suggestions about how preachers can prepare sermons that speak to children as well as to adults. It also includes suggestions on how preachers can encourage children to listen to sermons and how to help parents help their children listen to sermons.

You can preach to the kids, TOO!

Great, you say. I am already trying to preach to twenty-year-olds beginning their first jobs and retirees facing life without jobs, to people who just married, just divorced, or just buried a spouse, and that is just the beginning! You want me to add children to the list? Give me a break! But that is exactly what I want you to do—add them to the list. Recognize that they are there. Speak to their concerns, just as you speak to the concerns of everyone else. Many sermons or points within a sermon are directed to specific groups within the congregation. The rest of the congregation is invited to listen in and to make application to their own situations. I ask not that every sermon be focused on children, but that you preach with as much awareness of the children as of their elders. Learn a few new tricks that will invite them to tune in for at least a few minutes. Without totally revolutionizing your preaching style, you can preach to the kids, too.

1

Why Preach to the Children?

Why?

Why is it that way?

Why do you do that?

Why do I hafta?

Why can't it . . .?

Why can't I . . .?

Of all the many questions children ask, it is the why questions that tend to stump us. After too many why questions most adults eventually reply in exasperation, "I don't know. It just is." or "It doesn't matter. Just do it." Sometimes our "I don't know" is telling the truth. We really don't know. The children are asking a question that is beyond our knowledge. But sometimes the whole truth is "I don't know why and have given up the desire to find out" or "I think I know for myself, but I'm not sure I could put it into words—especially words that you could understand." It is these underlying "I don't knows" that lead us to say "It doesn't matter." And even as we say it, we know deep down that it really does matter. We just don't have the time, energy, knowledge, or inclination to explain why.

So, a book on preaching to children starts with the child's perennial question, *Why?* Why preach to the children? Let's begin by thinking from the preacher's point of view, "Why should I even try to preach to the children?" "The sermon is my best opportunity to try to reach and influence the adults, the leaders, the financial contributors in my church. These are people with big possibilities and intense needs. I need to give them my full attention and best efforts in the sermon." Preachers often think "Why should I try to preach to children? What do they need that I could possibly give within the framework of a sermon? Don't they get what they need in Sunday school?" These are important questions, questions we do not often stop to ponder. Our answers, or half-answers, or avoided answers, shape our preaching. So let's begin with the why question. "Why should we preach to the children?"

"Why? Do I Haf'ta?" Reasons for Not Preaching to Children

All right, let's take the part of the petulant questioner, who asks, "Why? Do I haf'ta?" Let's list reasons—and there are some very compelling ones—for simply deciding not to preach to the children. Most of these reasons sprout from the belief that sermons are actually for adults and that sermons and kids, especially today's kids, are basically incompatible.

1. Sermons are verbal. Children tend to be visual. Where else do children sit and listen to one person speak without interruption? Children grow up in a visual world. They watch television shows and videos. They listen to music with video accompaniment. So, they are ill prepared to listen to sermons.

Wait a minute! Isn't this also increasingly true of adults? None of us do much listening to uninterrupted speakers anymore. Even the TV news is mainly a series of images with commentary. Sermons ARE unique in our culture. Sermons are countercultural events by their format, no matter what their content. The question becomes not whether to expect children to listen, but at what age we can expect anyone to listen to a sermon and how can we teach visually oriented people to listen to sermons.

2. Sermons tend to be "long." Children have "short" attention spans. Those attention spans have been developed by years of watching rapid-fire television images and by education that often comes to them in a series of short blocks.

On the other hand, it is also true that children will devote uninterrupted hours to mastering a computer game, reading a book, or watching videos. The truth is that while our culture trains children to have short attention spans, most children are capable of longer spans of attention when their interest is focused and engaged.

3. Sermons tend to be abstract and general. Children tend toward the concrete and specific. Sermons tend to be filled with discussions of abstract religious concepts such as sin, forgiveness, justice, grace, and mercy. One way we try to preach to listeners with a variety of needs is to offer general truths that apply to many situations. This requires a fairly high level of thinking, which is possible for most adults. But studies of children's thinking patterns indicate that children are not developmentally capable of such thinking until their mid-teens at the earliest. Children think in specifics. They learn from specific examples rather than abstract generalizations.

4. Sermons ask us to think by sitting and listening. Children often do their best thinking when they are in action. They think with their eyes, fingers, feet, noses, and tongues. Most children's museums and classes invite children to think by working with materials. Children learn about the world by collecting specific experiences and knowledge.

Given these realities, even with mitigating circumstances, it is tempting to conclude that preaching and children are simply incompatible and that preaching is really an adult enterprise, and then follow one of these three options.

First, *dismiss the children. Send them out of the room to pursue activities that are more suited to their current abilities.* Congregations that follow this option offer church school classes, choir rehearsals, or children's worship services that replace the sermon with a story, a puppet show, a play, or some other child-focused presentation of the Word. These alternatives may replace the entire congregational worship service. Or, they may be offered only during the sermon with children leaving the sanctuary just before the sermon and, in some congregations, returning for the benediction. (One wag observes that this method teaches children to leave worship and that as soon as they are allowed to, they do just as they have been taught. They leave worship and never come back.)

A second option is to *include in the congregational worship service a short sermon designed especially for the children and then to direct the other sermon to the adults.* Following the children's sermon, children may leave the sanctuary to attend alternative activities during the adult sermon. Or, they may return to sit with their families and draw whatever they can from the longer sermon.

And of course there is the third option of simply *asking the children to sit quietly through the sermon and hope that they will grow accustomed to listening to sermons.*

Each of these options has merit. And each is pursued with varying degrees of success in many congregations. Chapter 2 is devoted to the possibilities and problems of the children's sermon. And our congregations are filled with sermon-listening adults who grew up in churches that used option three.

BUT . . . There Are Also Some Very Compelling Reasons to Include Children in Preaching

Current research into how children grow suggests that youngsters can benefit from listening to sermons as members of their congregation. And a significant study on the type of activities that lead to mature faith in adults found that children's participation with their families in worship is critical. Let's explore both the research conducted by human developmentalists and the findings of the Search Institute's seminal study of what contributes to the development of mature faith.

Faith Development and Listening to Sermons

A great deal of attention during this century has been devoted to discovering how people grow and develop. Distinct patterns have been identified in how people develop as thinkers, as personalities, even as moral decision makers and people of faith. These patterns have been described in academic books and given complicated abstract names.

John Westerhoff, in his book *Will Our Children Have Faith?* has summarized the findings related to faith development using the image of a tree. Westerhoff likens our faith to the trunk of a tree. He says that just as we cut across the trunk of a tree and see rings describing the seasons of that tree's growth, if we could cut across the trunk of our faith, we would see rings describing the seasons of our faith growth. Some trees would have lots of rings. Others would have only a few. But no matter how many rings any tree has, the rings would belong to four basic types: *experienced faith, affiliative (or belonging) faith, searching faith, and owned faith.* These faith types would be present in a unique pattern in each tree, but the overall sequence of rings in any tree would always maintain the order outlined above. In other words the heartwood of every tree is experienced faith, and in no tree would a ring of owned faith appear before each of the three other types of faith had appeared at least once.

At the core of every tree is the heartwood ring of *experienced faith.* One basic Judeo-Christian belief about God is that God comes into our lives. Our faith is not based on intellectual presuppositions, but on our encounters with God. The Bible is a record of those types of encounters. The history of the church is the story of how people have responded to their encounters with

God. It is the same in our individual lives. God starts not with our heads but with our lives. Our faith begins with experiences. People who become Christians as adults point to specific experiences in which they encountered God. Children of Christian parents begin life gathering experiences of being one of God's people. They pray the Lord's Prayer with the congregation before they fully understand every petition. They gather canned goods for the hungry before they appreciate the complex realities that contribute to world hunger. They are faithful by doing what God's people do before they can explain *why* they do what they do.

One of the things that Christians do is gather for worship and the preaching of the Word. Studying the Word and meditating on it together is considered a high privilege and responsibility among Protestants. Part of the Christian experience, therefore, is listening to sermons. For children (and adults) listening to sermons is one way to experience life among God's people.

The second ring of the faith tree is *affiliative (or belonging) faith.* People who live according to belonging faith live on the faith of the group. The group tells them who they are, what they believe, and how they act. Belonging faith is often perceived as negative because it is associated with the often destructive peer pressure of adolescence. But belonging faith can also be nourishing and healthy. When you meet an eight-year-old, the conversation usually begins with name, age, and grade in school. Next, the child will often list the groups to which she belongs. The unspoken assumption is that if you know she is a Scout and is on the express soccer team, you know who she is. If the conversation continues, she often displays caps, T-shirts, and other treasures that link her to her groups. She will tell you about the group's activities and what she does and does not do because she is a member of each group. She will tell stories about the group leaders who are special to her. To live on belonging faith is to be a full participant in the life and rituals of a group, to know and be known by the leaders of the group, and to accept the values and beliefs of the group as your own.

Belonging faith is not just for children. An adult, who when asked to explain predestination, responds, "well my pastor says . . ." is living on belonging faith. And most adults add sizable rings of belonging faith in the wake of life crises. "I don't know how I would have gotten through it without my church," they say. When they were too numb to think, the church was there with the rituals, the leaders, the hugs, and even the casseroles to carry them.

Worship is the heart of the life of the congregation. The sermon is where the congregation encounters and thinks about God's word together. A sermon is different from a class. In a sermon the whole congregation listens together. It's hard to imagine being part of a congregation with no knowledge of or involvement in what is preached. In the sermon the members of the congregation hear the group's leader explain the group's beliefs and values. The preacher models Christian behavior in what is said and how it is said. When my experiences and concerns are cited by the preacher, I know that they are valued by the group and I know that I am valued by the group. I know that the preacher wants me there and values my participation. Preaching can be an excellent way to nourish those who are living on belonging faith.

Searching faith is faith that doubts and struggles and questions. This type of faith is not possible for young children because they do not yet possess the mental ability for critical, abstract thought. That does not mean children do not ask questions—only that their questions are of a different kind. Children ask their questions with the assurance that we know the answers, and that if they can only stop us long enough, and make us explain it well enough, we can tell them all they want to know.

Searchers, on the other hand, are taking apart everything we have told them and evaluating it. When they ask questions, they do not care what we think. They are gathering grist for their own mental mills. Like teenagers who respond with endless "no's" and "I'll do it my way's" before they can stake out their own personal positions (which often reflect the positions of their group), searchers must evaluate everything the faith community has told them before they can make their own statements of faith. Searching is faithwork for adolescence and adulthood.

Preaching nourishes searchers by providing them clear

statements to evaluate. Preaching can also lift up searching as a noble and necessary Christian endeavor. The preacher who celebrates questions and tells stories of people asking tough faith questions both supports current searchers and suggests to future searchers that asking hard questions is part of being a Christian. Children thus come to expect rather than be frightened of facing hard questions.

The fourth type of faith is *owned faith*. A person living according to owned faith knows who she is, what she thinks, and what she must do. People living according to owned faith become uncomfortable when what the church preaches and what it does do not match. One excellent example of owned faith is Martin Luther standing before the gathered courts of both church and state, confronted with a pile of books and tracts he had written, and being ordered to retract them or face punishment. After thinking it over, Luther replied, "Here stand I. I can do no other. God help me. Amen."

Like searching faith, owned faith is not a faith option available to children. But sermons that include stories of people modeling owned faith teach children to grow toward owned faith.

Children live according to experience and belonging faith. So for them, listening to a sermon is what Christians do. Listening to sermons can also knit them more tightly to the community that is defining them. Listening to sermons can even point them to the faith road ahead.

The Search Report

Another recent study about faith development also suggests that participation in worship is important for children. *Effective Christian Education: A Study of Protestant Congregations,* known colloquially as the Search Report, asked what kinds of activities lead to the development of mature faith in adults. The researchers began with the following definition of mature faith:

A person with mature faith
1. trusts in God's saving grace and believes firmly in the humanity and divinity of Jesus;
2. experiences a sense of personal well-being, security, and peace;
3. integrates faith and life, seeing work, family, social relationships, and political choices as part of one's religious life;
4. seeks spiritual growth through study, reflection, prayer, and discussion with others;
5. seeks to be part of a community of believers in which people give witness to their faith and support and nourish one another;
6. holds life-affirming values, including commitment to racial and gender equality, affirmation of cultural and religious diversity, and a personal sense of responsibility for the welfare of others;
7. advocates social and global change to bring about greater social justice;
8. serves humanity, consistently and passionately, through acts of love and justice.

Next, researchers interviewed more than eleven thousand North American Protestants using two sets of questions. One set was designed to rank those interviewed on each of the eight characteristics of mature faith. The other was to identify the kinds of religious activities the interviewees had pursued throughout their lives to date. The findings were quite clear. Two things were shared by those who ranked high in faith maturity. First, they participated in Christian Education at all ages of their lives. Second, they tended to share four family experiences between birth and eighteen years of age. Those experiences are frequent conversations with Mom about her faith, frequent conversations with Dad about his faith, frequent family worship experiences, and frequent family helping projects.

Three of the four family experiences can be supported by the family's listening to and discussing sermons together. My experience is that children of sermon-loving adults tend to become sermon listeners. When an important adult in a child's life invites the child to worship—as an important experience that "I'm excited to share with you," children tend to give it a try. When conversations about sermons deal more with the content of the sermon than the behavior of the child, children tend to listen so that they have something to say later. That is why there's a whole chapter in this book devoted to helping parents welcome their children to worship and teaching their children how to listen to a sermon. It's not only important, but it is a task the church has failed to equip parents to undertake.

Children and the Mystery of God's Presence

One last thought about children listening to sermons comes from Sofia Cavaletti—a student of Dr. Maria Montessori who focused Montessori's methods on the religious development of children—and her students. Dr. Cavaletti insists that children have a God-given hunger for mystery and holy silence. She claims that despite our fast-paced, noisy culture, children respond to the opportunity to listen and to think quietly. Using Montessori methods, her students have developed worship experiences for children that insist on quiet, individual listening, thinking, and responding to biblical stories linked to the church year. Many Christian educators are at first skeptics, but as they experience this approach to worship with children, they come to appreciate the truth of its basic beliefs about children's hunger for silence and a sense of God's presence. Once those beliefs are claimed, the question becomes not whether children listen to preaching, but how we can preach to meet the needs of children as well as those of adults.

So, Why Preach to the Children?

Preach to the children because they need to experience hearing and thinking about God's Word as part of the congregation of God's people.

Preach to the children because they need to hear God's Word from the leader of their group (congregation), and with their group.

Preach to the children because they need to hear that their lives and their problems are part of the life and concerns of the whole congregation of God's people.

Preach to the children because God loves them and needs them to do the work of the Kingdom NOW. It is one thing to study the Word in Sunday school. It is another to be called, through preaching, to live out that Word as one of God's people.

Preach to the children because they want to be preached to. Elementary school–aged children are focused outward on the world. They come to worship ready to be full participants, and they want to understand. This will not last forever. During their teenage years their focus will shift to themselves and the world of their peers. If they have not grasped the significance of congregational life and worship by then, they are not likely to do so until their young adult years. This situation offers a window of opportunity between the ages of six and eleven when it is not only possible but highly desirable to help children become full participants in worship and yes, even to become sermon listeners.

The preacher's task then becomes one of gathering tools with which to address children as part of the whole congregation. The remainder of this book is a collection of such tools. Different preachers will find different tools useful. The expectation is that not every sermon will be 100 percent child-friendly, but that preachers will begin to recognize and preach to the children who are a part of their congregation. In turn, it is hoped that children will begin expecting to hear something in sermons that speaks to them and their situations.

2

The Children's Sermon vs. The Real Sermon

Time on the Steps, Special Time for Special Christians, A Moment with the Young Disciples, The Children's Sermon—this message addressed to children goes by many names. But in all cases it is a three- to five-minute block of time directed especially to the children. Often the children come to the front of the sanctuary and either sit with the preacher on the chancel steps or sit on the first pew with the preacher coming out of the pulpit to speak to them at a closer range. In this chapter it will be referred to as the children's sermon.

A survey of Presbyterian congregations indicates that the vast majority (82 percent), regardless of size or region in the United States, regularly include a children's sermon in Sunday morning worship. Experience indicates that this is true of most Protestant congregations in North America.

With the best of intentions congregations offer children's sermons as something for the children. Unfortunately, these pint-sized sermons bring problems as well as benefits, with the problems tending to outweigh the benefits. Let's explore both.

The Benefits of Children's Sermons

Children are important. "Children have a special place in this congregation. See, every Sunday we set aside time in our congregational worship especially for children." Congregations wanting to attract young families point to the children's sermon as proof that their children will be welcomed and well cared for. Congregations that are aging reassure themselves with the presence of children gathered around the pastor. "We're OK" they say to themselves. "Look at those wonderful children. They are the future of our church." For many adults in our age-segregated society, church is the only place they see children regularly. For some older adults and young adults, the children's sermon provides a much needed connection to children. The children's presence is a weekly demonstration of the theological truth that the phrase "God's people" includes people of all ages.

The children's sermon is a chance for the children to be physically close to and have the full attention of the pastor (the leader of the group), and thus feeds their belonging faith. When the pastor calls each child by name as they gather and speaks in their language about their concerns, children are knit into the community. When the preacher who has spoken to a child during the children's sermon invites her to pray with the rest of the congregation, she is ready to try out praying with her friend. When the pastor appears during a family crisis, children can receive her or him based on their experiences together during the children's sermons. When a child knows and is known by the preacher, he attributes to the preacher all he knows about the Christian community and attributes to the community all he shares with the preacher. So time spent up close and personal with the most important leader of the congregation knits the child into the congregation and into the family of God's people.

Of course the children's sermon is often the only part of worship that the pastor or the senior pastor (in a larger congregation) delegates. The intent of the pastor is to give the task to someone who can do it better, to give other staff people visibility, or to highlight the ministry of the laity. But for the children, the chance to be with the "leader" is lost. The unintended message is "you are not important enough to merit the attention and friendship of the leader of the group. He or she is really there for the adults. Others will take care of you until you grow up."

If the children come to the front, the children's sermon provides high energy children a "legal" opportunity to move around and stretch their legs a bit. Just walking down the aisle, sitting in a new seat, then walking back offers action-oriented muscles a break from the relative quiet of pew sitting. Every opportunity helps.

In many congregations, the children's sermon is a moment of relaxation, even laughter, for all worshipers. For those precious few minutes, standards are lowered, not just for the children, but for everyone. Everyone relaxes a bit, becomes willing to laugh, and enjoys being God's worshiping people. (An argument could be made that this might be reason enough to abolish children's sermons altogether since the real problem is that congregations need and want to laugh and relax during all parts of worship. However, laughter during the children's sermon lowers the pressure for laughter during the "real" sermon.)

Many adults say to the preacher, "I love the children's sermons. To tell you the truth, I get more out of them than I do out of the real sermon." They wink and smile when they say it, to assure the preacher that this is a compliment. This backhanded compliment actually stands between the benefits of the children's sermon and the problems with the children's sermon. The benefit is that adults enjoy them. But that benefit indicates two serious problems just behind the scenes.

The first problem is that a member of the intended adult audience for the "real" sermon is confessing that the adults' sermon is less memorable and "on target" for him than is the children's sermon. In other words, the "real" sermon needs work. It needs to be more like the children's sermon. It needs to be simpler, more specific, more story oriented, more relaxed, even more humorous.

The second problem is that what is offered to the children is often understood not by the children but by the adults. Children have very different experiences and thought processes than adults do. They think about the world and gather understanding of the world in unique ways. Many of the clever, cute children's sermons that are popular with adults do not honor these different ways of thinking.

For example, one very popular form of a children's lesson is the object lesson. An everyday object is produced to catch the children's attention and then is connected to a spiritual truth. At Pentecost a flashlight is produced and offered to a child to turn on. When it does not come on, the child and preacher identify the problem as a lack of batteries. The preacher produces batteries and the child turns on the flashlight. The preacher then compares our lives to the flashlight and points out our need to be powered by the Holy Spirit. Understanding this comparison requires symbolic thinking called transference. Teenagers and adults do it readily. Children do not. At the end of this sermon all the children know is that flashlights need batteries and the preacher thinks people need the Holy Spirit. They cannot connect these two facts.

The failings of this kind of thinking are illustrated by the story of the preacher who said to the children, "I'm thinking of something that is small, gray, furry, and likes to eat nuts." An eager five-year-old's hand shot into the air, followed by the words, "I know. I know." When called on by the preacher, the youngster said with enthusiastic certainty, "God! It must be God!" He then added with a sigh, "But it sure sounds like a squirrel to me." This five-year-old had figured out the object lesson format. But he hadn't a clue about the meaning of any one of the lessons. The thinking required was beyond his capabilities. If children's sermons are to reach the children, rather than the adults, they must be planned to fit a child's thought processes.

The Problems with Children's Sermons

Some of the benefits and the problems are subtly related. For example, the children's sermon does say to the children, "You are important." But it also says in two ways, **"You are different. You are not like the rest of us."**

First it says, "Your abilities and needs are different from those of the rest of us." This is true. It is also true that teenagers, forty-year-olds, and eighty-year-olds have different abilities and needs, but no preacher would consider asking all the forty-year-olds to come forward for a sermon addressed especially to them. It would be separating them from the congregation as a whole. It would embarrass them. So, why do we do it to children?

Second it says, "That was for you. Now sit down and be quiet (or go away) so we adults can have our time." In other words, sermons (and maybe all of worship) are really for adults. Children need not pay attention and actually do not belong here. Instead of inviting children to become sermon listeners, we say to them "the real sermon is going to be pretty awful. You won't be interested in it or be able to follow it. That's why we kindhearted adults have provided you with a children's sermon." If our ultimate goal is that children become sermon listeners, offering alternative children's sermons may be a shortsighted practice that actually hinders children from achieving the long-term goal. What we really want to do is help children listen to the *real* sermon.

Careful worship planners find that the children's sermon interrupts the flow of worship no matter where it is set. It inevitably feels like a break, an interruption, almost a commercial. When you traditionally move from praise to confession and assurance of pardon to proclaiming the Word to responding to the Word, you will find that anywhere you put a children's sermon will be an intrusion in the overall flow of worship. Even when it is set just before the sermon in the section on proclaiming the Word, it seems like a hiccup in the flow. The problem is that children's sermons are not part of the flow of worship for the entire congregation but are separate experiences included for one segment of the congregation.

It is difficult to preach to groups of children with a broad age span in the presence of adults and meet everyone's needs. It is not unusual to meet children as young as three and as old as nine on the chancel steps for the children's sermon. Those children worship in very different ways. Preschoolers respond to worship with their senses. They see, smell, touch, taste, and hear worship. They respond to the whole room and the people located there. They respond to the whole worship experience rather than to what is said or sung at any one time. They are looking for a feeling of welcome and for sensory experiences that inspire awe. Elementary schoolers need everything the preschoolers do, but they are ready to pay attention to specifics. Preschoolers respond to every sermon as an experience to be soaked up. Elementary schoolers, especially those who have become familiar with the sermon experience, are interested in the details of this sermon. They look forward to a good story or a good idea from the preacher. It is hard to meet both sets of needs in the same five-minute chunk of time. In one unfortunately common scenario, a question designed for interaction with an elementary school–aged child gets stolen by a preschooler hungry for loving attention, but with no idea about the details. The result is often a congregational laugh. The laugh may or may not meet the preschooler's need for loving attention, but it makes it nearly impossible to get back to the point for the older children. In the end, neither the younger nor the older child is served.

This situation leads to another problem with children's sermons. **They tend to exploit children.** Have you ever noticed that you never have to take a young person aside and say gently, "Don't you think it's about time that you stay in your pew and listen to the children's sermon from there?" Instead, before their parents feel the need to make this statement, children fold their arms across their chests and firmly declare, "I'm not going up there anymore." Behind their insistence that they are too grown up for that stuff is the refusal to be embarrassed by what can happen up there. They sense that they are being used for adult entertainment, not worship. If they are sitting in full view of the congregation on the steps, they get tired of being watched and realize that the preacher is often talking more to the folks in the pews than to the children on the steps. The congregational laughter makes them nervous. They know the congregation has laughed at normal-sounding answers offered by sincere children, and they dread the possibility that they will one day be laughed at in front of the entire church. Few adults would subject themselves to such a situation and once children figure out what is going on and find a way to escape, they will not be put in that position either.

The flip side of the exploitation problem is the child who manages to exploit the children's sermon for his or her own needs and desires. Some congregational laughs give instant birth to young comedians. Unfortunately, five-year-old comedians seldom have highly developed senses of what is appropriate. They are out for the laugh and are willing to risk almost anything to get it. These children often compete with the preacher for control of the congregation during the children's sermon. This is particularly funny for the congregation, at first, but painful for the preacher when the comedian is the preacher's son or daughter. Once such a competition starts, it is hard to stop and can make significant communication with children during the children's sermons impossible.

The Problems
DO Outweigh the Benefits

Children's sermons as practiced in most congregations tend to be most beneficial and enjoyable to parents and child-loving adults. These sermons meet congregational needs to celebrate the presence of children in the congregation. All intentions are honorable. But results do not live up to expectations. Children's sermons have little to do with the worship of God and are difficult formats in which to effectively proclaim God's Word to children. Children are set apart from rather than included in the congregation. They often feel exploited. Preachers find themselves saddled with a nearly impossible task of speaking meaningfully to children of many ages in a situation in which both preacher and children are on display.

Probably the most damaging product of the children's sermon is that after talking with the children, most preachers feel they have fulfilled their responsibility to the children and therefore totally ignore them in the "real" sermon. The question thus becomes, "At what age do we expect children to listen to that 'real' sermon?" The fact is that children do not suddenly one day listen to and understand a complete sermon. (Some adults never do this.) Instead, if the sermon includes some carefully planted tidbits to catch their interest, children will tune in for a while. Over the years, they tune in more and more frequently. So the trick to raising children who listen to sermons is not to provide them with an alternative sermon, but to seed the real sermon with stories, points, and language that catch their attention and teach them to expect that a sermon will have something in it for them.

But If You Must . . .

It is, however, not a perfect world. Sometimes the pressures to include children's sermons in congregational worship are so great that not including them causes more problems than including them. In such situations, try the following:

Preach to the children, not the adults. **Speak in their language about their concerns in ways that make sense to them given their thought patterns.** Avoid object lessons and moralizing. Instead, tell specific stories about particular people in particular situations.

Preach to the children, not the adults. **Position yourself so you can be close to the children and that *you*, rather than the congregation, can be the center of their attention.** If the children sit on the chancel steps, sit with them off to one side instead of in the center and encourage the children to turn toward you. Or kneel in front of them with your back to the congregation. If the children sit on the first pew, stand, sit in a chair, or kneel in front of them. (This is easier if there is no rail in front of the first pew.) In larger sanctuaries, a radio microphone is almost essential if the rest of the congregation is to listen in while the preacher maintains an "up close and personal" tone.

Use the children's sermon to explain windows, pictures, architecture, furniture, paraments, and sacred objects in the room. As you do, remember that children think very literally and specifically. They think of examples rather than generalities that connect examples. So a cross reminds them of Jesus and leads them to remember stories they know about Jesus. It does not remind them of God's forgiveness and never-ending love.

Use the children's sermon to teach children about different parts of worship. Rather than gathering the children at the same point in every service, gather them for the part of worship to be highlighted. After the congregation sings the doxology, invite the children forward to define "blessings" and to name some of the blessings that you and they receive. Then send them back to their seats and invite the whole congregation to sing the doxology again to thank God for their blessings. On another Sunday, just before singing a hymn, tell the children the story behind that hymn or explore the meaning of the hymn. Then send them back to their pews to sing the hymn with everyone.

If the children's sermon is moved around either to highlight the different parts of worship or as a way of presenting scripture, children will look forward to it. It becomes a treasure hunt that alerts the children to the whole worship experience and invites them to participate more fully. Once children are comfortable with this treasure hunt, it is possible to tell them occasionally at the beginning of the sermon that today's children's sermon is hidden in the sermon. Urge them to listen for it and tell you as they leave what it was. Then use at least one of the sermon ideas in chapter 5 in your sermon. Also be ready to be surprised by the different things children pick out from your sermon.

Use the children's sermon to teach children about the seasons of the church year. Point out the changing colors. Explain one chrismons ornament on the chrismons tree during each Sunday of Advent. Highlight a part of worship that is prominent during a given season. For example, during Lent highlight a prayer of confession by inviting the children forward, pointing out the prayer in the printed bulletin, putting some of the phrases of the prayer into children's language, and thinking about how children struggle with the sinful behavior confessed in the prayer. Then either send children back to their seats for the prayer or ask the children to lead the whole congregation in praying the prayer with you.

To draw children's attention to the scripture text for the day and invite them to listen to the sermon based on that scripture, **combine the children's sermon with the reading of the scripture.** As the children come forward, bring the big Bible down from the lectern or altar. Open it in your lap. Then introduce the text. Ask the children to imagine that they are the people who first listened to the text. For example, they can be the people gathered on a hillside on a sunny day to hear Jesus teach. Or they can be the fighting Corinthian Christians getting a letter from Paul. The preacher can stop reading occasionally to ask, "How did you feel when you heard Jesus say that?" or "Show me with your face how you felt when Paul said that part about . . . ." (Chapter 3 includes numerous suggestions for presenting scripture effectively to children. Though those ideas are at their best when used in reading scripture to the entire congregation, many of them can be used in creating scripture-based children's sermons.) You may simply read the text. Or you may explore one point about it that preaches especially to children. To really drive your point home and to encourage children to listen to sermons, refer to your children's sermon in the longer one, for example, "as I told the children . . ." or "as the children pointed out . . . ."

Plan a children's sermon that is closely related to the longer sermon. Use the children's sermon to set the stage for, make the first point of, or speak to children on the subject of the longer sermon. Use the children's sermon to define for the children a word that you will use repeatedly in the sermon. Then encourage them to listen for that word in the sermon. It is even possible to stop in the middle of the sermon to invite the children to the front, tell them what you've been talking about, make an explanation of the point especially for the children, then send them back to their seats with a suggestion about something to listen for in the next part of the sermon.

Finally and most important, remember that children's sermons that are an integral part of the morning worship

experience, *don't* **just happen.** It takes time to decide what to say and to plan how to say it. Preachers spend hours preparing twenty-minute sermons. Choirs spend at least an hour rehearsing a three-minute anthem. Liturgists think carefully about the day's prayers. Some even write their prayers out to get them just right. Children's sermons are no different. They require study, planning, even rehearsal. When children's sermons get that same amount of time and attention and are delivered by a preacher who loves children and is loved by the children, these sermons can be nourishing experiences for the children of the congregation.

THEN . . .

even though you are doing the children's sermon, preach to the kids in the real sermon. Use all the tools in the remainder of this book to invite and encourage and raise children to listen for God to speak to them in sermons.

3

Preparing to Preach to the Kids

Preparing to preach effectively to children does not mean finding "something for the kids" to add to the sermon you prepare for the adults. Instead, it means doing your entire sermon preparation aware that some of your listeners will be children. It begins as you study the text for the day or mull over the chosen topic, exploring its significance for children as well as for adults. It challenges you to give the sermon an outline and format that children can follow and to consider how your points speak to children. Imagine the children of the congregation looking over your shoulder as you work asking, "What will you say to us?"

This is really not as daunting as it sounds. It begins by asking three basic questions as you study the texts or explore the topic on which you will preach.

Question 1: What words does a child need to know in order to understand this text or topic? Words are the basic building blocks of a sermon. Not knowing or misunderstanding a key word is a major barrier to following a sermon. Unfortunately, many of the biblical words and faith words that are uttered in preaching do create barriers for children.

The church universal chuckles over the original way children hear some of the words of our faith. There is the child who prayed the Lord's Prayer, "Our Father who art in heaven, Harold be thy name . . ." while another prayed "Our Father who art in heaven, how d'ya know my name?" Funny? Yes, but these children could benefit from a little word study on that unfamiliar word, "hallowed."

Then there are the words whose current everyday usage is different from its biblical or faith usage. "Offense" is a good example. Most sports-conscious children define "offense" as the team with the ball. At church "offense" is another word for sin. So when we preach about forgiving offenses or forgiveness for our offenses, we need to explain just what constitutes an offense and why it needs forgiving.

To identify the words that need attention, read the biblical text(s) once looking specifically at the vocabulary. Read several translations looking for the words children will understand most readily. If you are starting from a topic rather than a text, make a list of key words you expect to use readily in the course of the sermon. Which words might pose problems for children? What could you do to eliminate those problems?

One preacher publicly collects "big words for Christians." Frequently during a sermon she will devote a few minutes to defining a word to be added to her collection. At times she recalls a word that is already in the collection and adds a new dimension to its meaning. Both adults and children enjoy this process and learn from it. Adults occasionally suggest words that need to be added to the collection.

Another useful device for exploring the meaning of words in preaching is to identify "used to thinks." For example, one nine-year-old reports that he "used to think" that God and Santa Claus were brothers, and that Santa lived at the North Pole and took requests for toys you needed at Christmas while God lived at the South Pole and took requests about what you needed during the rest of the year. Identifying the problems with this way of thinking and replacing it with new ideas about God does two things. First, it provides an opportunity to replace a rather childish understanding of how God responds to our requests. Second, it suggests that we keep growing in our understanding of

God. Publicly identifying common "used to thinks" about a variety of faith concepts leads listeners to expect that over time some of their current understandings will also become "used to thinks."

Question 2: Are there obsolete practices, beliefs, or cultural realities children need to explore before they can understand this topic/text? The Bible was set in a culture very different from the one in which children currently live. The biblical culture was mainly agrarian and local. The culture children live in today is mainly urban, technological, and increasingly global. Kids are interested in, even fascinated by, the differences in these two cultures. But they need help understanding the familiar aspects of the biblical culture.

Children need help understanding specific practices and items. For example, before children can ponder the good shepherd's careful watch over the sheep in the sheepfold, it helps to know what a sheepfold is. (To a child unfamiliar with sheep, a sheepfold can sound like a machine in which sheep are folded—like a paper folder.) Before the stories of the Samaritan woman at the well or the good Samaritan make full sense, children need to know about the tensions between Jews and Samaritans.

They also need help with more general assumptions that have now changed. For example, much of Paul's talk about atonement presupposes an understanding of the ritual of sacrificing animals at religious temples. People in Paul's day routinely practiced such sacrifices to honor their gods. But animal sacrifices intended to honor God or to ask for God's forgiveness probably make no sense to children living in the twentieth century. Children, and often adults as well, need help in understanding how such disgarded past practices hold truths that are still important for us now.

Question 3: What does this text or topic say to children? *If your starting point is a text,* read it once from the point of view of a child. What interests you about the characters? What do you think they looked like? Do you like and trust them? Or do they seem dangerous to you? If you could meet them, what questions would you ask them and what advice would you want to give them? Would you want them as friends or leaders? Why? What about the plot grabs your attention? At what point in the plot do you want to know what happened next? Does anything happen that is very different from your experience? If so, what do you need to know before you can believe that it happened and understand how it happened?

Children prefer stories to essays. But many biblical essays are part of larger stories, for example, Paul's long theological letters are responses to problems in particular churches. When children know the problems the texts address, they can listen to Paul's ideas and evaluate their usefulness in solving the problem in the original church and in solving similar problems today. This is easier if the problem is one they recognize as currently existing. For example, the bickering Christians of the church in Corinth will grab the attention of children more quickly than the Christians in Ephesus worrying about eating meat offered to idols.

What does the scripture say to you? Try summarizing the message of the story or essay for an eight-year-old. Does it make sense? Is it meaningful to an eight-year-old in your church or city? Is it good news for that eight-year-old? How do you feel when you hear from a child's perspective?

Some texts feel very different to adults and children. Abraham's near sacrifice of his son Isaac at God's request is one example. Adults, hearing the story from Abraham's point of view, are impressed by Abraham's faith and reassured by God's not requiring the sacrifice of Isaac. Children, hearing the story from Isaac's point of view, are frightened. How could God ask a parent to do such a thing? What if there had been a mistake and Abraham had not been stopped in time? How did Isaac feel when his father tied him up on that altar? If God asked my parents to kill me, would they? Children need to be told clearly that Isaac was never in danger, that God loved Isaac and was protecting him. They also need to know that many religions at that time required parents to kill their firstborn child as a gift to their god. The God of Abraham did not and would not require this sacrifice—not then, not now, not ever.

BIBLE STORIES THAT OFFEND CHILDREN
(BUT NOT ADULTS[*])

[*]Some texts offend both children and adults because they challenge what we think and want. These stories offend children because children hear them from a child's point of view rather than an adult's point of view.

The Story	The Problem
Cain and Abel	Why did God refuse Cain's sacrifice but accept Abel's? Unless there was a good reason, I'd be mad too.
The Flood	Why should God kill all the animals because the people were bad? That was not fair to the animals!
Abraham almost sacrifices Isaac	How could God ask a father to do that? If God asked my parents to kill me, would they?
Ishmael and Hagar sent away	That was not fair to Ishmael and Hagar. They shouldn't have to suffer just because God chose Isaac.
All stories in which oldest inherits all	(especially if the listener is not the eldest child) That's not fair!
God kills the firstborn in Egypt	(especially if the listener is the eldest child) Why did God kill the firstborn to get at Pharaoh? The children had done nothing wrong!
Samuel in the Temple	Poor Samuel! Imagine living all alone in the Temple and seeing your parents only once a year and getting only one set of new clothes each year!
"But I say, . . . if you are angry with a brother or sister . . ."	Hey wait! Everyone is telling me it is OK to be angry. I just have to learn to deal with angry feelings without hurting anyone. This must be wrong!
"Whoever loves son or daughter more than me is not worthy . . ."	But I depend on my parents entirely. Please, God, don't make them choose between me and you!

Some texts seen from a child's point of view offer insights that enrich everyone's understanding of the text. When adults read about the healing of Naaman, they tend to focus on the seven baths in the muddy Jordan River as God's chosen means of healing. When children read the story they are delighted by God's choice of a little slave girl as the bearer of the critical piece of information that enables the cure. They are pleased that her mistress and master take her information seriously and act on it. The story promises them that God takes children seriously and that children can make important contributions now.

If your starting point is a high holy day, think about that day from a child's perspective. During **Advent and Christmas** children are facing all the traditions of the season without the instruction they used to get in the public schools. For better or worse, they are more dependent on the church and their families to tell them the stories and introduce them to the carols. Preachers must assume much less knowledge on the part of their young listeners. The Christmas stories, however, present few special problems for children.

Easter, on the other hand, demands that different approaches be used for people of different ages. Adults respond enthusiastically to the Easter claim and promise of victory over death because adults understand the finality of death and fear death. Children, however, have a hard time grasping the reality, especially the finality, of death. Even after attending Grandpa's funeral and seeing his casket lowered into the ground, a child will often want to know when Grandpa will be visiting. This natural inability to grasp the finality of death is supported by fairy tale princesses who awaken after "sleeping" for years; by cartoon characters who, flattened by steamrollers, peel themselves off the road; and by superheroes who, though apparently dead, revive to fight again. Given all this, it's not surprising that children can't get too excited by victory over death.

Recognizing this situation, much of the current Easter curriculum and worship resources for children focus on new life, paying special attention to eggs, bulbs, butterflies, and other symbols of new life. Children, however, are only vaguely interested in these symbols. "New life" strikes few of them as particularly significant or exciting since all of life is "new" for them.

The more helpful Easter messages are found in the biblical stories. To younger children, the empty tomb story is the ultimate victory of the good guys (God/Jesus) over the bad guys (Judas, the priests, Pilate, the soldiers). On Good Friday the bad guys thought they had won. They killed Jesus and sealed his body into a guarded tomb. On Easter morning God/Jesus blasted right out of that tomb and proved once and for all that God is more powerful than even the worst evil the worst bad guys can inflict. The natural response to such a victory is to yell "Hooray for God and Jesus!" and to celebrate belonging to God who is the most awesome power there is in the universe!

To older elementary school–aged children, who are focused on friendships and have clear expectations of "best friends," the most significant resurrection story is the story of Peter's breakfast conversation with Jesus. Peter had been Jesus' best friend. He had promised to stick with Jesus no matter what. But he had been caught three times on the same night pretending that he did not even know Jesus. Such betrayal by a "best friend" deserved condemnation then as it would now. As a betrayed "best friend," Jesus would have been justified in ignoring or punishing Peter for his denials. But Jesus did not. For Peter, the Resurrection happened when Jesus forgave him, welcomed him back as a friend, and put him to work building God's kingdom. For older children, Easter holds the promise that Jesus will forgive them and welcome them back even if they betray their friendship with him. Such Easter forgiveness is worth celebrating!

And then there is **Pentecost.** Pentecost is one holy day that has not been taken over by commercial interests. Many congregations actually overlook this day. But more and more congregations are finding it significant. It is in many ways the birthday of the church. It is also a celebration of the Holy Spirit, of God's presence with us. Children are fascinated by both aspects of Pentecost. They love birthdays with all the traditions and talk of "the day you were born" and "how you have grown." Many churches incorporate children's birthday rituals into a birthday party for the church that begins in worship and continues with a cake and punch party afterward.

Preaching on that day often takes one of two directions. It can focus on the church—both the church universal and the individual congregation—and can be an opportunity to remind listeners of the true identity of the church while helping the congregation evaluate its effectiveness in living up to that identity. Sermons that offer specific examples and activities that include children will help youngsters "listen" to talk about the church on its birthday.

Or the sermon can focus on God's presence. One question children often ask is "How can you tell when God is around?" "God is with us all the time," is the typical answer, but this response does not completely satisfy young questioners. When children read stories from the Bible about God speaking through burning bushes, angels, or the wind and flames of Pentecost, they often conclude that either God has quit talking to people in such obvious ways or that God has decided not to talk to them personally in those ways. In either case, they are disappointed and a little miffed with God. Pentecost is an opportunity to describe in great detail some of the everyday ways people sense God's presence with them. Pointing out that some people sense God with them when they are outdoors, others while listening to or playing music, some during quiet times of prayer, still others while they are doing God's work, some when they are worshiping, others when they are alone, and so forth helps children identify experiences in which they have sensed God with them. Using lots of stories to which listeners of all ages might respond with "something like that happened to me" can be most helpful for understanding Pentecost.

Whether you are starting with a text, a topic, or a holy day, think about children early in the process of preparing the sermon.

An Alternative Approach: Start with the Children

On the Sunday that a group of sixth and seventh graders was to be confirmed, one preacher began his sermon, "I usually preach mainly to the adults and hope that the kids find some worthwhile ideas in what I say. Today I am going to preach to the kids, mainly to the kids who are being confirmed, and hope that the adults find some worthwhile ideas in what I say." He then preached a serious sermon about knowing who we are. The message affirmed that we are God's children, created in God's image and called to be a part of God's kingdom. He urged us all not to listen to those who tell us that we are worthless or who want us to settle for being less than God created us to be. Instead of his usually erudite references to current books and events, he told stories using athletics and talked about being judged by teachers, coaches, and friends. Listeners of all ages insist it was one of his very best sermons. The children felt loved and respected and left with a message that was particularly relevant to their lives that week. They, as individuals, and their concerns had been taken seriously. The adult members of the congregation, who also struggle with maintaining a sense of self, felt they had heard a valuable message well worth taking home. They were able to readily add their own experiences with judgmental supervisors and coworkers to the preacher's accounts of judgmental teachers.

Children face many critical times through which the church has an opportunity, even a responsibility, to help them navigate. Most of these times focus on faith themes that we continue to wrestle with throughout our lives.

For instance, **the first day of school** is an intense time for children. There is the challenge of new classes, new teachers, new friends, maybe even new schools and new ways of getting to those schools. For many, there are new clothes and new books. The excitement spills over into the entire culture making the first of September more the beginning of the new year than January 1. September is a time of getting back to work after summer vacations. Community and church organizations and clubs begin new rounds of activities in September. Many lectionaries recognize this with texts about renewed commitment and discipleship. All of this suggests "Back to School Sermons" that explore both the excitement and fears of new things and call children to be God's people in their new classes and activities.

(Warning: Remember the children who do not do well in school because of academic problems or because they are not accepted by their classmates. For them the return to school is a reminder of last year's failures and therefore they are filled with dread for the upcoming year. Adults tend to talk to these kids as if this year will be different, that all the children will start the year "even," and that any child can succeed with a little hard work. After a few years, children who have fallen behind academically or who are repeatedly ostracized at school know better and, unable to share in the hype, begin the year feeling lonely and even more hopeless. These children need to hear that their predicament is recognized. The children who study with learning disabilities and other challenges need the support of their church. Those who feel like outsiders need a warm welcome at church. They also need to hear all children encouraged to reach out to them at school.)

Report card time is a recurring judgment day for almost all children. Those who do not do their best fear the demands for better grades. Those who are not academically gifted but did their best, and those whose lives are consumed by problems that make schoolwork difficult fear that even their best will be found "not good enough." Both the A student and the marginal student fear being judged as "not good enough." So report card time is an ideal time to explore God's insistence on saving us rather than judging us. It is also a time to explore the different gifts God gives each of us and to explore the tension between trying hard to be a good disciple and knowing that God loves us no matter how well we do.

The **end of the school year** is filled with as much intensity as its beginning. Most children are ready for a change of pace. They want to be done with homework and being indoors. Some are looking forward to summer trips, camps, and sports. Others are worrying about new challenges. Going away to camp, changes in day care arrangements for children of working parents, and more time spent dealing with other children in the neighborhood can cause as much apprehension as anticipation. Sermons that talk about how God's presence is with us everywhere—on sports fields and beaches, as well as in classrooms, will help children deal with these changes.

Halloween, though it seems a secular holiday to most adults, can be a high holy day for children. Basically it is an opportunity to face our worst fears with the realization that God is with us and protects us. During Halloween, elementary school–aged children try to survive scary stories and walks through haunted houses, and enjoy dressing up as monsters (finding them not so scary after all!). It is important to them to prove themselves brave. One preaching opportunity is to point out that God is more powerful than any monster or evil power and that God is with us even in the scariest situations. The key text for this point is Romans 8:38-39. Children (and adults) can be armed with that text and sent out to stand up to any scary thing that they encounter.

Super Bowl Sunday, the World Series, the NCAA basketball playoffs, and a host of local and regional sports and school-related championships for a time each year dominate the attention of many children. "We're Number 1!" they chant with excitement untempered by the knowledge that next year someone else will be Number 1 and in a few years only the most dedicated fans will recall who won the championship in which year. Their enthusiasm is often fed by media hype, and by their developmental need to make peace between the warring urges within to compete and to cooperate. Sermons about who is Number 1 in Jesus' book, and sermons that compare the value of proving your own greatness versus caring for others help children develop solid Christian attitudes toward competition in our very competitive society.

Infant baptism, first communion, and confirmation are intensely interesting to children because they are public celebrations marking the growth of children. Children can remember or anticipate their turn at each one. On the Sunday that one of these rituals occurs, children are primed to hear the stories behind and the meaning of that ritual. By preaching a sermon about that ritual, pastors take advantage of a great educational opportunity for the whole congregation.

When sermon preparation begins with situations that children encounter and uses the language and stories that children recognize, we generally address issues with which adults still struggle. And while children do not have the experiences and mental ability to adapt what is said about adult realities to their childhood situations, adults do have the experience and ability to apply what is said about children's realities to their adult situations. So occasionally preaching from a child's perspective is one way to effectively reach both children and adults.

4

Presenting Scripture So Children Can "Hear"

Worship planners who follow lectionaries begin with the scriptures for the day and build the sermon and liturgy around them. Other worship planners start with an idea or theme that grows from scripture and build the service from there. In either situation, the scripture is critical. Worshipers who do not "hear" or understand the scripture miss an important key to the whole service.

Actually, they miss more than the key to one specific worship service. They miss an opportunity to encounter God's word through scripture. Christians sometimes describe themselves as "people of the book." We live our lives in response to the God we encounter in the Scriptures. Given that, it's not surprising that the more ways we hear scripture, the more powerful a place scripture occupies in our lives. Scripture-loving adults often refer to particular readings or presentations of a text that brought the words to life or gave them new meaning. Watching a play based on a biblical story or hearing the Holy Week stories read as candles are extinguished on Good Friday help us "hear" God speak through the Scriptures in ways we miss by simply reading the passages. So one way to proclaim God's Word in worship is to present scripture in a variety of well-thought-out powerful ways.

Given the importance of the reading of scripture to worship it is strange that the scripture reading often gets less time and preparation than any other part of worship. Frequently, the worship leader simply reads from his or her favorite translation or from whatever translation is provided in the pews. People who refuse to speak or pray in public can generally be persuaded to read the scripture with the comment, "All you have to do is read it."

Therefore, a chapter on presenting scripture effectively is included in a book on preaching in the belief that children's interest in and invitation into the sermon often begins with well-presented scripture text. When children witness scripture presented powerfully, they pay attention and are primed to hear more. For that reason we need to move from "reading" scripture to "presenting" scripture. The same studious and creative energy can be devoted to presentation of scripture as is given to the sermon. In this chapter you will find a collection of ways to present scripture effectively in the setting of the congregation's worship. Basically there are two steps: first, choose what is to be read with an awareness that some of the listeners are children with limited verbal abilities; and second, plan a lively presentation of the text.

STEP ONE: Choose the translation with the children in mind. One of the blessings of living in this century is accessibility to many high quality English translations of the Bible. Most Bible students have their personal favorites, but each translation offers unique strengths and weaknesses. Part of the preacher's task is to select the translation that most clearly presents the text for the day. The phrasing of a particular verse or the choice of words can make a significant difference in how a passage is understood or if it is understood at all. Adults may stumble over unfamiliar words but can often get past them to the meaning of the sentence. Children, on the other hand, can be stopped cold by unfamiliar words. So when choosing a translation to use for any given text, think first about the children.

Choose texts with familiar words. For example, compare these versions of Psalm 1:1.

BLESSED is the man that walketh not in the counsel of the ungodly, nor standeth in the way of sinners, nor sitteth in the seat of the scornful. (KJV)

Happy are those who do not follow the advice of the wicked, or take the path that sinners tread, or sit in the seat of scoffers. (NRSV)

Happy are those who reject the advice of evil people, who do not follow the example of sinners or join those who have no use for God. (GNB)

The first translation, the King James Version, with all the "th's" on the end of words, is difficult but not impossible for children to follow. In fact, most children have no trouble with the first two lines in any of these translations. It is the vocabulary in the last phrase that dictates the choice. Neither "scornful" nor "scoffers" are commonly used words. Most children have no idea what they mean, and without understanding these words, the meaning of the phrase is lost. "Those who have no use for God" is much clearer.

Also, look for words with both literal and symbolic meaning. Remember that children think literally and therefore can be thrown off by symbolic meanings. So if the choices for Romans 12:1 are: "Therefore, I urge you, brothers, in view of God's mercy, to offer your bodies as living sacrifices, holy and pleasing to God" (NIV) and "So then, my brothers, because of God's great mercy to us I appeal to you: Offer yourselves as a living sacrifice to God, dedicated to his service and pleasing to him" (GNB), choose the latter. Adults may know that Paul is not literally asking for each person to be killed on an altar for God, but children do not.

Finally, watch for big, abstract words. In some services you may want to use a word or phrase repeatedly in order to define it and help build the congregation's understanding of the term. In other instances you may want to choose the translation that avoids the difficult vocabulary in order to focus on another message. In the case of the latter you might choose the *Good News Bible* for 2 Corinthians 5:18, "All this is done by God, who through Christ changed us from enemies into his friends and gave us the task of making others his friends also" rather than the New Revised Standard Version's "All this is from God, who reconciled us to himself through Christ, and has given us the ministry of reconciliation."

Finally, there are certain texts that the congregation knows and loves in a specific translation. Though that translation may not employ the most child-friendly language, the children will sense its importance to the people around them. So when the choice is between the King James Version's "THE LORD is my shepherd; I shall not want" and the *Good News Bible*'s "The LORD is my shepherd; I have everything I need" most readers will choose the familiar and loved King James Version.

No one translation is always the best choice for children. Each has strengths and weaknesses. The *Good News Bible* has been targeted to a fifth-grade reading level and everyday late-twentieth-century American English vocabulary usage. However, it is not always the best choice for a given text being read in a service built around a given theme. So the first task in presenting scripture is to choose carefully the translation that best communicates the day's text—and to make that choice with special sensitivity to children's verbal limitations.

STEP TWO: Plan an appropriate presentation of the text. It is often said that the Bible is a library composed of many kinds of literature—poetry, stories, court records, letters, prophetic writings, histories. But in public worship we tend to read the Bible as if it were an encyclopedia. One reader reads every text in majestic, modulated tones.

Children, however, listen for more than the context of the words. They gather the meaning of the text from the person reading, the feelings being expressed, and the way the reading is presented. If the words and the way they are read do not match, children do not believe what they hear. Passionate psalms read with sonorous respect don't make sense. Confrontations read in a monotone are disregarded. Therefore, if we want children to listen, we need to present scripture in ways that communicate what God is really saying. We must "present" the text, not just "read" it. We need to pay attention to and highlight all the riches within the texts. The possibilities for doing this are numerous.

We can match a reader or readers to the text. Ask a teenage girl and an older man to read the songs of Mary and Zechariah. Solicit a twelve-year-old boy to read the story of Jesus in the Temple at age twelve. Plan for an older couple to read one of the stories about Abraham and Sarah. Coach a young man to read John the Baptist's words with all the fire that John employed.

A presenter can also assume the role of the speaker or writer of scripture. No matter how dissimilar he or she is to the biblical writer/speaker, the presenter can adopt a voice tone, facial expression, posture, and even hand movements to help listeners "hear" what is going on. Yell out the words of the prophets and point your finger like they did. Use a whiny voice to read the complaints of the psalmists. Let your voice and face explode with the incredible joy of Moses and Miriam as they danced on the far shores of the Reed Sea.

It is also possible for one person to adopt the postures, voices, and tones of several people. For example, in presenting Jesus' story of the Pharisee and the tax collector, a reader can rise to her full height, puff out her chest, and speak in pompous tones when describing and quoting the Pharisee, then shrink, drop her head, and almost whisper when describing and quoting the tax collector.

This can even be done in presenting the many extended conversations that appear throughout the scripture. The presenter steps to one side of the lectern, turning slightly toward the center to read one role, then steps to the other side, turning back toward the center to read the other role, and later stands at the center facing forward to read any narration. For example, in presenting one of Jesus' many confrontations with the Pharisees, the presenter steps slightly to one side of the lectern, facing a bit toward the center and adopts a proud prose and pretentious tone to read the words of the Pharisees, then steps slightly to the other side of the lectern again facing toward the center and assuming a more open, gentle pose and tone to read the words of Jesus. The narrator's words are read from the center of the lectern facing forward. (Omit the "he said's" and "she said's" within the conversation to achieve a smooth flow of conversation.)

When the presenter assumes the role of the speaker or speakers, children, who because of their limited verbal skills listen with their eyes and hear tones as well as words, understand more fully what the scripture is about.

It is often helpful to involve more than one person in presenting scripture. Dialogues, for example, can be presented by one person assuming the different roles. But they are often more effective when different readers assume the various roles. When these readers are well rehearsed, listeners feel as if they are eavesdropping on the conversation. Many stories involve extended complex conversations. In these cases readers' theater helps everyone keep up with what is going on and what is being felt. If the people "reading" the various characters in Jesus' story about the rich man and Lazarus stand in appropriate positions on the chancel steps to read, the action as well as the feelings become clearer. For the most part, older youth and adults, rather than children, read the parts in readers' theater. Even so, this adult presentation brings the scripture to life for the children.

The need for multiple readers in a dialogue is obvious, but other texts sometimes suggest more than one reader. Often during worship, we read a series of related short parables, teachings, proverbs, and stories. Having each item in the series read by a different person helps children recognize the separate items. So when reading a section of the Sermon on the Mount that includes several of the "hard sayings" of Jesus or when reading a series of short parables, have different people read each saying or parable.

Set the scene and invite listeners into it. Describe the situation and assign listeners a role to play. Tell them about the situation of the church in Corinth, then invite them to pretend they are members of that church and are hearing Paul's letter for the first time. Describe the miseries of life in exile, then ask the congregation to imagine themselves as captives in Babylon hearing Isaiah's prophecy of hope. *The Revised Common Lectionary* pairs the story of the earthquake that released Paul from prison with Psalm 97 implying that Psalm 97 was the kind of psalm Paul and Silas might have been singing that night in prison. After reading about the earthquake, instruct people to hold their wrists out in front of them as if they were handcuffed together. Have them imagine that their hands were chained to the wall and that they had been beaten that day along with Paul and Silas, then read the psalm of happy praise the way Paul might have recited it. Another idea is to introduce Daniel and his captured friends, then challenge the congregation to listen for the risk those teenage boys took with their food.

The shape of a poem must be considered in presenting it well. All of the psalms and Lamentations, most of Job, much prophecy, and many other texts are poetry. Each poem has a poetic shape that helps communicate its meaning. It is helpful to highlight that shape in presenting the poem.

Psalm 1 offers sharply contrasting descriptions of "good" people (verses 1-3 and 6*a*) and "bad" people (verses 4-5 and 6*b*). When the psalm is read by two people taking the two parts, the contrast is emphasized. The two readers may stand apart or may stand back-to-back at the center of the chancel with each turning to face the congregation to read or recite "his or her" verses then returning to the back-to-back position while the other speaks.

Psalm 24 is a call to worship with groups of people, who ask questions that are answered by others. The situation comes to life when the verses are read responsively by groups of people at the front and the rear of the sanctuary. Groups that are already in place, such as the choir at the front of the church and the ushers at the back, can take these parts, or special groups can be formed for the reading.

There are fourteen acrostics, or alphabet poems, in the Bible. Each verse or section of verses in an acrostic begins with succeeding letters of the Hebrew alphabet. The result is a series of poetic lines loosely related to the same theme. When acrostics are read by one reader, the psalms seem to ramble and lack logic. To help the congregation "hear" the psalms as they were intended, either ask one reader to call out the appropriate Hebrew letter before each verse as it is read by another reader, or have each verse read by a different person who says the Hebrew letter before reading or reciting a particular verse. (*The New Jerusalem Bible* prints the English alliteration of the Hebrew letter in the margin beside the appropriate verse.) To grasp the effect, read through a portion of Psalm 145. Then imagine a group of older children standing in a line across the front of the sanctuary with each child calling out his letter and reciting his verse in order.

THE ABCs OF THE BIBLICAL ACROSTICS

Nahum 1:2-8	An alphabet poem about Yahweh's wrath begins Nahum's prophecy against Nineveh.
Lamentations 1–4	Four of the five laments over the fall of Jerusalem are alphabet poems composed in the ruins.
Proverbs 31:10-31	An alphabetical description of a good wife.
Psalms 9–10	Prayers for deliverance
25	Prayers for deliverance
34	Imagine David's followers calling out the letters of the alphabet with David replying with a praise for God that begins with that letter. What a way to demonstrate his sanity and celebrate his escape from Abimelech by pretending insanity!
37	Encouragement to trust God even when it looks like evil succeeds
111	A poem praising the great historical deeds of Yahweh
112	Description of the rewards of living a righteous life
119	The longest psalm praises God's Law. Eight verses begin with each letter of the Hebrew alphabet.
145	An alphabet poem praising God
Ecclesiasticus 51:13-30	A life spent seeking wisdom

Many psalms have subtitles, marginal notes, or commentary notes that suggest how the psalm could be presented. Psalm 107, for example, is a song that was sung by religious pilgrims as they walked toward Jerusalem. Verses 1-3 are an introduction, which is followed by "verses" each describing the troubles of a group of people who cried to God for help and were rescued (travelers, prisoners, the sick, and seafarers), and then concludes with a hymn of praise. It is not unlike some of the seemingly endless songs families and youth groups sing on long car trips. This comes to life when the psalm is presented by a group reading verses 1-3 in unison with the verses that describe troubles represented as solos that are being interrupted by the group's recurring refrain (see verses 6 and 8, 13 and 15, and so forth).

In colonial America when books were scarce, psalms were frequently lined out; that is, a leader read a line and the congregation repeated it. The leader read another line and the congregation repeated it. And so forth. If psalms are lined out in a monotone, the practice is deadly dull. But if the leader reads dynamically and invites the congregation to repeat the dynamics as well as the words, the feeling of the poet is often highlighted and shared.

Pantomiming (having a story acted out as it is read) is an effective way to present some texts. Pantomiming serves two purposes. First, it helps listeners follow stories that involve complex actions. In Acts 15 people and letters are exchanged as the early church tries to settle a disagreement. It is easier to follow the action if people carrying big letter-props move about in the chancel between city signs, thus illustrating with their movements what the presenter is reading. The second purpose of pantomiming is to enrich passages that describe rich, complex emotional situations with very few words. The story of Mary and Martha is a fine example. Much is assumed in this terse account. When the story is only read, children miss many of the assumptions. But when it is pantomimed by two women who can show with their faces and bodies some of the feelings between the sisters, the situation is understood. Children, who are expert at reading faces, say to themselves, "Ooh, I've seen Mother look that way. We've got trouble here!"

Children are able to pantomime stories to clarify the action. Youth and adults will need to pantomime situations that involve complex emotions. Children simply do not have the experience to do the latter.

When introducing a congregation to pantomiming scripture it is often best to ask adults to lead the way. A scripture well pantomimed by adults will be welcomed as an inclusion of art in worship. Later, a pantomimed presentation of scripture by the children will be considered by the congregation as a way of including the children's artistic gifts to worship. However, if the children pantomime first, the congregation may perceive pantomiming as a cute, but not always welcome way to include children in worship, and few adults will subsequently agree to pantomime stories, even stories with obvious adult content.

It is also possible to draw listeners' attention to a text with props. Before reading a text, produce an object that will be featured in the text, and urge people to listen for the mention of that article.

Before reading Amos 7, dangle a plumb line over the pulpit and demonstrate its use. If possible, leave the plumb line hanging over the pulpit in full view. Instruct worshipers to listen for how God and Amos used a plumb line to warn the people of God. Then read the text.

Jesus used a mustard seed as a prop. To follow his lead, tape one mustard seed in each bulletin. A children's class can often be enlisted for the taping and then thanked publicly when the seeds are first mentioned in worship.

One preacher in a large church used worshipers as props. He prepared the congregation for the reading of the parable of the lost sheep by asking one hundred people to come to the front of the church. He counted them off loudly and touched each one as they came forward. At first, mainly children came forward but then some adults realized they would also be needed and joined the crowd. Soon the front of the sanctuary was packed. Once he reached one hundred, the preacher said, "One hundred is a lot of people! Today we are going to read a story about a shepherd who has one hundred sheep. Thank you for helping us all know how many sheep that man had. Return to your seats and listen for God's Word."

An old calligraphy pen helps both the reader and the congregation hear the epistles. Paul, especially, tended toward long rambling sentences that are difficult to read aloud. One way to help listeners better understand these passages is for the reader to introduce the text as part of a letter, display the pen, and then use it while pretending to write the letter while reading the text aloud. This is particularly effective if the reader imagines that he or she is the writer and shows the thought processes with facial expressions, verbal tones, and even pauses as if thinking while writing.

Most lecterns and pulpits include a railing or ledge on which such props can be prominently displayed. Props can be left in place for the duration of the service and may be referred to in the sermon. If such a railing is not available, the altar, communion table, or a small pedestal table can be used.

Some Practical Observations

"Presenting" instead of "reading scripture" is a good opportunity to include a variety of people in the worship service. Individuals can be called on to do very specific jobs that fit their gifts and abilities. Groups, such as Sunday school classes of all ages, choirs, youth groups, drama groups, or scripture study groups can be asked to prepare a specific reading.

"Presenting" instead of "reading scripture" requires practice. At the very least, an experienced presenter has to rehearse different expressions, tones, and motions aloud. When novice presenters are included, they will need to practice speaking from the front of the sanctuary. If there is a sound system, they may need instructions on how to use the microphone, and become accustomed to hearing their voices through the system. Children need to be forewarned that it will feel and sound different when the room is full of people. Multiple presenters will need time to practice together.

Although this method of presenting scripture requires more effort, there are a multitude of payoffs. First and perhaps most important, the scripture will become more alive and understandable for the children (and everyone else). Second, when a growing number of people in the service, worship is perceived as community property rather than the preacher's private turf. Third, as children see themselves and others presenting scripture, they feel more at home with worship in general and scripture in particular. God's story becomes "my story." And finally, having "heard" the scripture, children are primed to at least wonder what the preacher will say about it. Hearing the scripture is the beginning of hearing the sermon.

5

Shaping a Sermon That Children Can Follow

Once we have studied the scripture for the day from the perspectives of children as well as adults, and have presented it to the congregation in an inviting way, it is time to preach. The question becomes, "How can we shape sermons that draw the attention of children as well as adults?"

Our visual culture does not make it easy for anyone to listen to one person speak for an extended time. Children frequently watch television programs that are divided into short, snappy bites. Most children are watching TV and videos before they are able to read books. Many prefer videos to books after they have learned to read. In school they seldom listen to the teacher talk for extended periods of time, since the emphasis is on participatory learning featuring small-group tasks, workbooks, and class activities in near rapid-fire succession. This means that part of the challenge of preaching to children is helping them learn how to listen to one person speak for an extended period of time.

When I observe people listening to sermons, I see few children (or adults) listen to an entire sermon. Instead they tend to tune in as they hear things that catch their attention, and stay tuned in until one of two things happens. Either they lose interest because they cannot understand what is being said or because what is being said is beyond their interest and experience. Or they hear the preacher say something that speaks directly to them, which starts them thinking about a specific personal concern. In the former case, they rejoin the preacher if a new point recaptures their attention. In the latter case, they rejoin the preacher when they come to the end of their own thoughts or when the preacher interrupts them.

Given this, the preacher's aim is to help the children tune in more often and stay tuned in longer. There are lots of strategies for achieving this aim, most of which fall into two general approaches. The first approach is to shape the whole sermon in a way that helps the children comprehend the overall picture. The second is to scatter "hooks" throughout a sermon that are designed to draw children in for at least a little bit. Both approaches have great value, but the different strategies are most effective with different types of sermons.

When a Sermon Is a Series of Points . . .

One straightforward way to help children follow the preacher through a sermon is to **give them the outline in advance.** This need not give away all that is to come, but simply alerts them to some things to listen for. A well-known preacher began his sermon in a large congregation this way, "I want to start with a hint to my young listeners. You can keep up with me if you listen for a bear, a basket, and a party, in that order." The items appeared in stories he told to illustrate points as he worked through his sermon. As each item was mentioned, children's heads bobbed up all around the sanctuary. Many parents and children exchanged knowing looks. For the children who were least interested, the three items provided a gauge to their "how long till this is over" question. But even they were pleasantly surprised that the preacher thought enough of their presence to provide a hint about what was going on in the sermon. For some it was their first indication that they might want to listen to, rather than simply endure, any sermon. The children who were more involved listened to learn about the bear, the basket, and the party. They tuned in to the message as long as they could follow what was being said, then tuned out until the next item was mentioned. Because the bear, the basket, and the party were each tied to one of the main points of the sermon, they helped children understand those points.

A second way to ensure that children understand each point is to **introduce each point with the same phrase.** Martin Luther King Jr. did this powerfully in his "I Have a Dream" speech. He began each point in his agenda with "I have a dream." Listeners of all ages paid special attention each time he restated that phrase. They may have missed some of the details, but each time he called out, "I have a dream" they knew he was going to say something new and important, so they listened. Such repeated phrases call attention to each point as it is made, and tie the points together with a common theme.

A third way the preacher may help children keep track of the points in a sermon is by **developing a dramatic device to emphasize the introduction of a new point.** One preacher with the daunting task of preaching after lunch on a particularly difficult passage from one of Paul's letters, set the sermon up as a conversation with Paul. He began by saying that when he got to heaven, he wanted to have a long talk with the apostle Paul. There were some questions the preacher very much wanted to ask Paul. He thought he knew what Paul would say, but he was looking forward to finding out for sure. Then he staged the conversation as he imagined it. He presented his questions from one side of the pulpit. When he turned to speak as Paul, he moved to the other side of the pulpit. As one might expect in a conversation with Paul, there was not a lot of back and forth. After the preacher asked each of his four questions, Paul unloaded a fairly lengthy answer. The result was that every time the preacher changed position and assumed his questioner voice, listeners were alerted to expect a new question and a new point. Each time a new question was posed, listeners who had tuned out were invited back into the sermon.

Not all sermon points are best presented as ideas. It is possible, even desirable in this visual age, to **organize a sermon around a series of mental pictures.** Thomas H. Troeger in *Imagining a*

Sermon offers two examples of wedding sermons. One focuses on explaining each of the promises made in the wedding vows. The phrase "promise and covenant" is used repeatedly. The other tells of a couple who takes a photo of themselves in their wedding clothes on each anniversary. In the process of describing the taking of these pictures over the years, the preacher illustrates how the couple keeps their wedding promises. Both sermons preach the same message. But because the second sermon tells a story and deals with specific people in recognizable situations, it invites children to listen and keeps them listening. The first sermon, on the other hand, tends to lose them with generalities and big words.

There will also be times when many points in a particular sermon speak more to adults than to children, so **develop one point that speaks specifically to children so that it will draw their attention.** Illustrate that point with stories from childhood or from children's literature or videos. Use props or refer to familiar objects. This is rather like nesting a children's sermon in the middle of the larger sermon—the advantage being that children who are expecting that the sermon will include something for them will slowly learn to listen to all sermons.

When a Sermon Follows a Text . . .

One classic sermon format is to work through a text verse by verse, or phrase by phrase, explaining what is being said and exhorting listeners to apply the message to their lives. This format provides listeners with a clear understanding of what the preacher is doing and where we are in the sermon at any given time. To offer even more help, direct worshipers to **follow along in their Bibles.** If people are not likely to have Bibles with them and there are no pew Bibles, print the text in the worship bulletin.

Point out specific words and phrases from the text. If you refer to other passages, instruct the congregation to hold a finger in one place and turn to the next passage. Give page numbers to help young readers (and adults who may have trouble finding their way around the Bible). The physical activity of finding words and phrases, following the preacher's progress through the printed text, and flipping to other pages helps children stay with the preacher and hear what is being said. Following along in the Bible gives children a satisfying sense of having listened to an entire sermon—even if in reality they missed some of the preacher's points. The sense of satisfaction leads them to want to listen to other sermons.

When the Sermon Is in the First Person . . .

Use a sermon format other than "talking about" an idea or text. To invite children to listen, **take a role other than that of preacher.** On Stewardship Sunday take the role of a coach giving a pep talk to his team. After reading a part of one of Paul's letters to an early church, assume the roles of several church members discussing and responding to what Paul wrote. If the day's text is a story, assume the role of one of the story's characters and reflect on what happened, how you feel about it, what you learned from it, and what you will do as a result of what has happened. In each case, become that person. Adopt mannerisms, ways of speaking, and even introduce props that the person might have used. Offer a thought-provoking dramatic monologue or dialogue. Even if they do not catch every point you make, the children will likely listen longer to hear what you are doing, and they may learn that sermons can be interesting—even when you don't understand them completely. Later, they may have fun calling you by the name of the character you assumed—as a way of showing that they listened and to build their friendship with you, their preacher.

Using Your Voice As a "Hook"

Finally, children do not listen only to words. They listen to voices. They follow the voice as much as they do the content of the sermon. So one way to keep their attention and to lead them through a sermon is to **use your voice in a variety of ways.** One preacher has suggested that every sermon has a voice as well as a content outline. If you are to draw listeners in, the voice outline must be as interesting and persuasive as the content outline. There will need to be both quiet, reflective comments and loud, fiery pronouncements. There can be thoughtful pauses, and times when the preacher is talking so fast and intently that listeners have to pay attention in order to keep up.

Many preachers begin their ministry by preaching in a variety of natural voices just as they would in conversation. Unfortunately, over the years, a "preaching voice" develops that reflects their expectations of what preaching ought to sound like. Nearly all of these "preaching voices" mask, rather than enhance, the preacher's message and they tend to lull listeners, especially children, to sleep. Changes in volume, speed, and tone of voice alert listeners that something new is happening and invite those whose minds have wandered to rejoin the preacher.

In this chapter I presented my outline at the beginning, emphasized my points with bold type, and gave examples from sermons that I have heard. I could have shared portions of conversations that I have had with children about sermons they remember. Or I could have chosen one text and offered several ways to preach it to the kids as well as to the adults. Each of the different strategies would have appealed to a different group of readers. It is the same way with sermon-shaping strategies. Each one fits some texts better than others. Each has value. Variety is key. When children come to sermon time asking, "What will it be this week?" or "What will happen next?" or "When is the part about the . . . ?" they have come to expect that sermons have something to offer them. So they listen—at least some of the time. And that is the beginning of being able to hear God speak through the Word as it is preached.

6

Choosing Illustrations That Draw Children In

No matter how they are shaped, most sermons include several stories and references to books, current events, and cultural situations. Generally, these serve as illustrations for points the preacher is making. They also connect biblical truths with the everyday life situations being experienced by members of the congregation. Carefully chosen illustrations make a difference in how well listeners understand the preacher's point and how they can apply that point to their lives.

Often listeners, who have tuned out, tune back in when the preacher mentions a book they have read, a movie they have seen, a community situation they are involved in, or an everyday life story. Once tuned in to the illustration, they stick with the preacher for the point that is being made. So carefully chosen illustrations often make the difference in how much of the sermon is actually heard by the majority of listeners.

When preachers cite only illustrations from the world of adulthood, they leave the children out. But when preachers cite illustrations from childhood (as well as from adulthood), children listen. Indeed, children often first pay attention to a sermon when they hear the preacher mention something with which they are familiar. They stick with the preacher until the general, abstract talk loses them. So if sermons are seeded with illustrations that catch the attention of children, children pay attention. They begin to expect that sermons will include stories and ideas of interest to them. As they are better able to follow the abstract talk that occurs between the illustrations, they listen to more and more of the sermon until one day they surprise themselves with the realization that they have listened to an entire sermon.

Illustrations that attract children's attention and those that attract adult attention are not mutually exclusive. There are two kinds of illustrations that attract and speak to both children and adults. These are stories about childhood and incidents from classic children's stories that people of all ages know.

Illustrations from Childhood

The one thing that every member of the congregation has in common is that everyone either is or has been a child. Everyone knows what it is like to wait for a test grade, deal with a bully, feel lost, or finally be able to do something that seemed impossible (jump off the diving board or say your part in a program). When childhood experiences are mentioned in sermons, children say, "I know about that. The preacher is talking to me." Adults say both, "I remember that!" and "That is not all that different from what happens to me now. The preacher is talking to me." This recognition makes childhood experiences a very useful source of sermon illustrations.

Stories from childhood can be used throughout a sermon to illustrate specific points. For example, in an Advent sermon on repenting, stories about children making changes in how they treat difficult neighbors, teachers, or classmates can be mixed in with calls to change the way we speak about and treat political adversaries. When illustrations from childhood are exactly on target, children may get the preacher's point from the story rather than the talk that surrounds it. If the point is not completely obvious in the story, interest in the story may spur young listeners to try to follow the preacher beyond the story to the point of the sermon.

One preacher often begins sermons with a series of stories from different stages of life. For example, a sermon about discipleship during the summer began by describing children singing "school's out, school's out, teacher let the monkeys out" on the last day of school, teenagers dreaming of spending their days at the beach, and adults hanging on by their fingernails for the relief they hope will come with a summer vacation from their jobs. Listeners were grinning or rolling their eyes at one another as they recognized themselves and members of their families. He then used the details from those scenes to talk about what people really want and need during the summer to bring true "re-creation" and to point out some summer dead ends. Most children listened to the introductory scenes. Many tuned back in every time one of the scenes that interested them was mentioned again. A few were drawn in by the everyday life stories and listened to the majority of the sermon.

Using childhood illustrations also has two pitfalls. First, it is essential to tell real stories about real kids. "Cute" or "idealized" stories about children are as offensive to children as glossed over, unrealistic stories about supposedly "real" adults are to adults. One ten-year-old, upon hearing in poetic detail about a boy out frolicking with his dog on a crisp, sunny autumn day turned to his mother and expressed his reaction with the infamous finger-down-the-throat sign. His mother was embarrassed, but everyone around him smiled. The kid was right.

The other pitfall is telling stories about your own children. Preachers' kids cite this as one of the most frightening parts of being the child of a pastor. Hearing Mom or Dad say, "when Sharon . . ." produces deep primal fear. No one wants his or her life continually used as an example for the whole community. Preachers' children are no different. So remember your children's experiences and use them to "make up" tales about fictional kids. Or if you must tell a story, get the child's permission first. But as a general rule do not tell stories—even complimentary ones—about your children from the pulpit.

Alert preachers who live with children have ready access to the world of children and thus to illustrations from that world. Preachers who do not have regular contact with children can stay abreast of the world of children by reading books about children. While books for adults about children are helpful in outlining the needs and problems of children, and frequently include stories about particular children, books for children about other children generally do a better job of describing the details of children's lives, feelings, and problems.

Beverly Cleary wrote a series of children's books that capture the joys and sorrows of a girl named Ramona as she grows up. The books were written some time ago and therefore are dated; for example, Ramona's ten-year-old friend Henry gets his first job delivering newspapers in his neighborhood. But the vast majority of the situations that occur at home and school in the books happen in the lives of real children today.

Judy Blume is a more recent author. *Tales of a Fourth Grade Nothing* and *Superfudge* tell funny, real stories of the problems of Peter Hatch and his little brother. *Are You There God? It's Me, Margaret* describes the woes of Margaret during her sixth-grade year in a new school. *Blubber, Then Again Maybe I Won't,* and *It's Not the End of the World* are a few of Blume's other books that describe very common childhood experiences.

All of these books are available in the children's section of public libraries. They are quick, entertaining reading, and they provide a wealth of tales about children and are reminders of usable tales from your own childhood. To locate even more such books, make friends with a children's librarian, bookstore owner, or elementary schoolteacher. Enlist their help in pointing you toward books that describe childhood events with truthful clarity. Also consider cultivating a fun and productive partnership with an avid young reader. Tell him that it helps you preach well if you know what children are reading. Keep up with what he is reading. Ask him particularly to tell you about good books about children. Discuss what he likes and dislikes about the books he mentions.

Below is a list of common childhood experiences that will help prod your memory. Read it reflectively with a pencil in hand. As you read, recall specific examples of the experiences that you yourself have encountered or heard about from others. Make notes in the margin. As others experiences come to mind, add them to your notes. The goal is to begin paying as much attention to the experiences and feelings that children cope with as you do to the issues, realities, and feelings that adults cope with. Keeping the list handy to work on over a couple of months can be a great continuing education project for preachers who feel they are out of touch with childhood.

Childhood Experiences with Gospel Connections

Family

—good times

> happy vacations
> peaceful eras when everyone was happy
> special meals
> holidays, birthdays, celebrations of achievements
> being tucked in bed at night
> the power was off, and we had fun being stranded together
> reunions or visits with much loved, but seldom seen extended family

—bad times

> the weather was bad, everyone wanted to do something different and bickered
> we wanted to watch different TV shows at the same time
> the backseat of the car on a long trip: "She's on my side!"
> bad weather kept us all cooped up inside for days
> illness—
> > one person critically ill
> > everyone got the flu at once

—siblings

> sharing a room with a line drawn down the middle

"She's got in my stuff and ruined it!" (usually the older)

"He's a baby and he's always in the way!" (the older)

"He's a bully. He never shares. He's mean!" (the younger)

"Does she have to go with me? She always does something embarrassing."

"They (my parents) love the others more than they love me."

"I'll never be as smart, pretty, athletic, and so on as he" or "How can anyone as smart, pretty, athletic, and so on as me have a sister who is completely hopeless! She can't do anything!"

—family crises

divorce

new child is born or adopted

elderly relative moves in

a job is lost

eviction

death or critical illness

family moves

house fire

Clothes, toys, possessions

having a wonderful dress or shirt you love to wear

having to wear something you do not like

hand-me-downs (both the great and the awful)

wanting something "everyone else has"

a loved toy is left in the rain or the driveway and is ruined

School

new school, new teachers, new buses, new rules and expectations

first day at kindergarten, middle school, or new school

teachers you love, teachers you don't like, teachers who don't like you

"hard" subjects: "I just CAN'T do it!"

waiting for report cards, test grades, project grades

who sits where in the lunchroom and on the bus; and
who works together on projects

being held back, having to go to summer school or have
a tutor

winning or losing elections

Friends

the joys of a best friend who shares everything with you,
even dressing alike

the agony of betrayal by a friend who goes with new
friend or group

a friend tells your secret with embarrassing results

the pain caused by exclusive child-created clubs or
cliques

standing up to friend for "what is right"

the love of a pet, a doll, or stuffed animal who is a best
friend

an imaginary friend

coping with a bully

tattling

Fears

the dark or monsters hiding in the dark

being left or lost in a strange place

fierce animals (wild bears or the scary-to-me cat next
door)

storms

the fears of death that develop after the death of someone
important, for example:

fear that a parent (or the other parent) will also die

fear of own death, even distrusting the dependability
of anyone or anything

parents will divorce

being a victim of violence at home, at school, or in the
community

Stewardship/Responsibility for others

taking care of a pet

baby-sitting; being left in charge of younger siblings

standing up for children who are getting teased/tricked
by others

giving time/money to a service project

championing efforts to save the environment, for
example, anti-litter campaigns

General

"It's NOT fair!"

making sure you get your fair share of cookies, toys,
time, everything

living with (and breaking) rules

understanding and coping with punishment

"Am I Number One?" "Am I good enough?"

winning or losing the game, the prize, the election

getting chosen first/getting chosen last

you're the hero who made the winning play or the goat
who lost the game

failing in front of friends

learning to make choices and live with the consequences

"I never thought she'd do that when I . . . !"

"I know I said I wanted it . . . but now . . ."

doing something the first time, for example, going away
to camp

performing: a championship game, a part in a play, a
recital, doing a feat, for example, breaking the board at
karate class

moving or having a best friend move

Illustrations from Children's Classics

The other source of sermon illustrations that both adults and children appreciate is children's classics. Most adults, even those without children of their own, have either seen as a child or escorted children to see the Disney animated films and other classics. These stories are common property. We all remember, or can call to memory, Pinocchio's lie detector–nose. Most of these tales have become classics because they deal with human dilemmas that are common to all people at all stages of life and in all times of history. That means many of them have great potential as sermon illustrations.

In order to mine these stories for sermon illustrations, begin with the characters. Often there are clearly drawn villains, heroes, and heroines. Identify what makes each one particularly evil or good. Review biblical history for similar characters. Cruella DeVille, the puppy-fur coat loving villain in *101 Dalmatians,* is a soul mate with the vineyard stealing, murderous Queen Jezebel. Ask yourself what habits or characteristics of that person Christians ought to cultivate or avoid. For example, Cinderella managed to forgive her selfish stepsisters and stepmother many times every day for offenses that are familiar, but I hope not as common, to all families.

Then familiarize yourself with the plot. What problems do the characters face, how do the characters solve them, and what might we learn from this? In *Aladdin,* with its powerful sorcerers and genies, the major problems are solved by plain people using their very human abilities. This fact is a good reminder to Christians who would like God to solve their problems like a benevolent magician, and is a spur to help us use the gifts God has given us to tackle the problems we face.

Some stories are filled with sermon illustrations. Others offer only one or two. Cinderella's problem (getting to the ball) and its solution (the magical work of a fairy godmother) do not lend themselves to preaching, but her ability to forgive does. On the other hand, none of the characters in *Aladdin* are particularly useful, but the way they use their own human abilities to solve the problems they face encourages us to do likewise. In some stories it is the story as a whole that offers illustrations. In others it is specific scenes within the story that preachers find useful.

There is one warning about using these stories. Adult minds move nimbly from topic to topic, making brief references to related topics understandable, even a way to add richness to a sermon. Children, however, think in a more focused way and need time to recall the details of the situation mentioned. If you say, "Just like Snow White's vain stepmother, we look into our mirrors comparing our beauty to everyone else's and hope we are the 'fairest one of all' . . ." the adults remember the infamous mirror and move on to what is being said about us. Children however need more. Children, having heard the statement above, perk up halfway through the next sentence to whisper loudly, "What was that about Snow White?" Children need to hear the story of the wicked Queen and her conversation with the mirror in some detail. Only after they have rehearsed and relished the Queen's vanity are they ready to think about how we might be like that Queen. So the warning is to take time to unpack illustrations from children's literature. Do not just mention them in passing.

Consider devoting continuing education time to reading and viewing children's classics to accumulate a wealth of sermon illustrations that speak to both children and adults. Get a head start on this assignment with the outlines of preaching points in several of the best-known children's classics that appear at the end of this chapter. To add to the list, ask for other suggestions from children and the owners of video rental stores that cater to children.

An aside? When I told a group of neighborhood children that I was preparing the following list, they were thoughtfully silent at first. Then one asked somewhat incredulously, "You mean for preachers, like at church?" A parent standing nearby summed up her negative expectations with a sermon-wise roll of the eyes and a rather sarcastic, "Right!" Then a seven-year-old disappeared into her house, returning in less than five minutes with a pile of eight of her favorite videos for me to watch. They are all on the list below. Unlike her mother, she has great expectations for the possibilities.

A Preacher's Guide to Children's Films/Videos We've All Seen

Aladdin. This movie is most remembered by adults for the hilarious performance of Robin Williams's genie. But the basic story is about two young people, Aladdin (the "street rat") and Jasmine (the princess who must be married off), who want a chance to live fully. They both want to love and be loved and to explore the world. The theme song suggests that people are not always what they seem and that we should not be fooled by appearances. Zacchaeus, Levi, Martha's sister Mary, Joseph, Ruth, the boy David, and all the other overlooked people in the Bible understand the problem and cry out for people to recognize in them the image of God.

It is also interesting that in a story featuring dueling sorcerers, it is people without any special powers who finally solve the big problems. At the end, the foolish sultan decides that since he is sultan, he can change the law that says a princess must marry a prince, thus enabling Jasmine and Aladdin to marry. Aladdin, using his own wits, defeats Jafar by tricking him into wishing himself into a genie's confining bottle. David when facing Goliath, Daniel in the lions' den, and Queen Esther also found that God gives us what we need in order to deal with the problems that come our way.

Bambi. This is primarily a story about community and growing up. It features a community of animals: Bambi and his parents, Thumper (a rabbit), Flower (a skunk), the wise Owl, and a host of unnamed animals. The story highlights young animals playing together and adult animals taking care of their young and one another. The animals all gather to see the newly born (similar to scenes in *The Lion King*). The young discover their similarities and differences. (Thumper, who could run at birth, comments about Bambi, "He's kind o' wobbly, isn't he?" to which his mother replies by asking him gently but firmly, "Thumper, what did your father tell you this morning?" Thumper replies, "If you can't say something nice, don't say anything at all.") A young adult Bambi takes on a pack of dogs who are attacking his doe friend Feleen. His father stops his own flight from the forest fire to help the injured Bambi escape too.

Flower's name provides an interesting parallel to all the naming stories in the Bible (Abraham and Sarah, Isaac, Naomi to Mara, Simon to Peter). Bambi, upon meeting the skunk for the first time in a clump of flowers, mistakenly names him "Flower." At first, Thumper laughs at the obvious incongruity, but Flower, also laughing, happily accepts the name that defines him positively and later responds by giving his child the name of Bambi. Names can limit, alienate, or inspire. In this case, the names draw the community closer together.

If this story has a villain it is "man" (this *is* an early fifties movie!). Whenever "man" comes into the forest, trouble follows. There is seemingly indiscriminate hunting and an unguarded campfire that turns into a forest fire. The picture is very much the opposite of the Genesis picture in which "man" is given care and protection of the garden.

Cinderella. Cinderella's father dies, thus leaving her in the care of a stepmother who shoves her aside to servant status while doting on her own daughters, Anastasia and Druscilla. The story begins by stating that Cinderella remained kind, patient, and good to everyone because she met every day with hope. Each day she is an example of forgiving love—forgiving her obnoxious, demanding stepsisters at least seven times seventy times.

The Hunchback of Notre Dame. Disney takes great liberties with the original story. The story Disney presents has many of the original characters and several preachable scenes and themes. Frollo, Quasimodo's master, is a villain whose evil is prejudice. He sees all gypsies and peasants as less than human. He kills Quasimodo's mother, tries to kill Quasimodo, but is stopped by the bishop, and sets fire to a house in which he has barricaded an entire family all without a qualm. Even though he is attracted to Esmeralda's beauty, Frollo cannot see her strength and goodness. Rather than try to win her love, he uses his power to force her to choose between death at the stake and being his mistress. As usual, prejudice causes nothing but problems and unhappiness for everyone.

A recurring song asks, "What is a monster? What is a man?" calling viewers to compare the physically monstrous Quasimodo and the morally monstrous Frollo.

While taking sanctuary in the cathedral, Esmeralda sings a prayer not for herself (though she is in great danger), but for all the outcasts of the world, while other more respectable worshipers pray "bless ME" with wealth, health, and love. The parallels to Jesus' parable of the Pharisee and the tax collector are obvious.

Lady and the Tramp. Lady is a cocker spaniel who learns the lesson many children have to learn, that there is enough love in a family for everyone—even when a new baby is added. (Jesus also had trouble teaching people that God's love was not limited.)

When Aunt Sarah and her two Siamese cats arrive to take care of the baby while Lady's owners, Jim Dear and Darling, are on vacation, Lady finds herself the object of Aunt Sarah's prejudice against dogs and her preference for her cats. When Aunt Sarah muzzles her, Lady runs away and is rescued from a pack of dogs and befriended by Tramp, a mutt. When Lady loyally returns home, she is chained to a stake in the yard. From there she sees a rat heading for the baby's nursery. Her barking brings Tramp who then rescues the baby, but is caught and sent to the pound by Aunt Sarah. When Jim Dear and Darling return they find the rat and figure out what has happened. Tramp is rescued and added to the family. Aunt Sarah's treatment of dogs is one example of how prejudice is played out. It parallels biblical stories about people prejudiced against foreigners, Samaritans, and Gentiles. It also parallels Frollo's prejudice (in *The Hunchback of Notre Dame*) against gypsies. Parallels to current prejudices also abound.

The Lion King. Scar, King Mufasa's brother, uses Simba (Mufasa's son) as bait to lure King Mufasa into a trap in which Scar kills him and takes over as king. Young Simba is sent off to sure death with the idea that he caused his father's death. Simba is rescued by a warthog (Pumbaa) and a weasel (Timon), while Scar, in cahoots with the hyenas, despoils the kingdom of the lions. Once Simba grows up, he must face up to who he is, fight Scar, and take his place as the rightful king. The preaching connections are in specific scenes rather than the general story.

1. The movie begins and ends with the presentation of the son of the current lion king to all the animals. It is very much like infant baptism. The child/cub is held up before the gathered crowd to be recognized and welcomed. Everyone there promises love and protection for the youngster.

2. When Mufasa speaks from the stars to Simba when Simba is deciding whether to return and challenge Scar, he says,

"Remember. Remember who you are. You are my son and the one true king." In many ways we are called to remember who we are—the true children of God—and to act accordingly.

3. Mufasa provides an excellent example of a parent's love for a child when he jumps into a wildebeest stampede to rescue Simba. God loves us like a lion parent who risks his life in a stampede in order to rescue a cub.

The Little Mermaid. This is a child's version of the tale of Faust. Ariel, a teenage mermaid, gives up her best gift (her beautiful voice) to get from the evil sea witch Ursula her biggest dream—the chance to be human and win the love of the handsome prince she saved in a shipwreck. What she does not know is that the prince remembers only her voice. So when Ursula appears in the form of a young girl with Ariel's voice, Ariel fails to win the prince's love. Only intervention by her powerful father and fast-thinking friends saves her and her father's kingdom.

1. The point to ponder is the danger of making highly questionable, even dangerous trades to get what we want. Ariel knew she was taking a very dangerous risk with a person she knew to be evil. But she did it to get something she wanted badly. In this case she was lucky, but there were some very close calls.

2. Ursula the seawitch is another picture of evil incarnate. She wanted power. She wanted to rule the sea and would do anything at all to get what she wanted. She had no concern for anyone or anything else.

101 Dalmatians. When Pongo and Perdita's fifteen puppies disappear, the search leads to the discovery of ninety-nine dalmatian puppies that Cruella DeVille has hoarded to make into fur coats for herself.

1. Absolute evil incarnated in the person of Cruella DeVille who "worships" furs and would go to any ends to acquire her obsession of a dalmatian puppy fur coat. Her evil compares well with Queen Jezebel, Herod killing all the babies in Bethlehem, the Roman emperors killing Christians, and so forth.

2. It took everyone working together to rescue the puppies: the dogs of the Twilight Bark alerted animals for miles around and located the puppies; a cat helped them escape from the DeVille place; a horse temporarily stopped the thieves who pursued them, the cows fed them when they were hungry. (It was practically an animal Underground Railroad.)

3. One hundred one dalmatians is a lot of dogs. Recall scenes of puppies everywhere. Then tell the parable about the shepherd with one hundred sheep.

Pinocchio. Pinocchio was a wooden puppet whose quest to become a real boy was aided by Jiminy Cricket (his conscience) and the Blue Fairy. (Real boys are brave, truthful, and unselfish.)

1. Pinocchio's nose grew every time he told a lie, which led the Blue Fairy to comment, "a lie keeps growing and growing until it's as plain as the nose on your face."

2. Jiminy Cricket quickly explained that a conscience is "that still small voice that people won't listen to" then tried to explain temptation to Pinocchio thus,

Jiminy Cricket: The world is full of temptations!
Pinocchio: Temptations?
Jiminy Cricket: Yep. Temptations. The wrong things that seem right at the time but . . . even though . . . the things may seem wrong, sometimes the wrong things may be right at the wrong times . . . or . . . a . . . vice-versa. . . . Understand? (talking faster and looking more confused as he goes)
Pinocchio: But I'm going to do right!

3. The coachman collecting bad boys for the trip to Pleasure Island said, "Give a bad boy enough rope and he'll soon make a jackass out of himself." At Pleasure Island boys could do whatever they wanted and did become jackasses.

Snow White. This story offers the preacher one vivid character, again an evil one—Snow White's wicked stepmother, the Queen. Her sin is vanity. She could not stand for anyone to be more beautiful than she. She regularly asked her magic mirror, "Mirror, mirror, on the wall, who is the fairest one of all?" When the mirror replied that Snow White rather than she was fairest, the Queen vowed to kill Snow White. She died in the attempt when a rock she was trying to push down a hill onto the pursuing dwarfs fell on her instead.

This list includes only Disney animated classics. That is just one subset of the vast collection of well-known and loved children's film/video classics. Just as there are few adult films that have absolutely no preaching potential, most children's films also contain preaching possibilities. So the challenge (or maybe the delightful excuse) is for preachers to know these works well enough to use incidents and characters from them to illustrate preaching points.

One aside about some currently popular television shows and movies. *The Teenage Mutant Ninja Turtles* are four charming, oversized, pizza-loving turtles (Leonardo, Raphael, Michaelangelo, and Donatello) spawned in nuclear slime and trained in the martial arts by "Old Rat." Their endless adventures pit them against a recurring villain named Shredder. No matter what the problem the Ninja Turtles punch and kick their way out of it, leaving Shredder and his evil gangs nearly dead but able to rise again for the next episode. *The Power Rangers* are a more recent version of the Ninja Turtles. In these stories the heroes and heroines are human teenagers who are transformed into powerful Rangers, each attired in a different colored uniform. Like the Ninja Turtles, they physically fight their way out of encounters with a variety of evil powers. Both the Ninja Turtles and the Power Rangers are child versions of every adult little-guy-defeats-the-evil-powers-by-persistence-and-lots-of-violence movie. Both are the antithesis of Jesus' calls to loving enemies into friends.

7

Using Sermon Props

Edgar Dale, a professor of education at Ohio State University, has done studies on how much people retain of the content they encounter. His findings were presented in a famous chart known as Dale's Cone of Learning. Imagine that the rectangular frame of the chart is the content a person is communicating, the amount within the central cone is the amount that is retained, and the area outside the cone represents the amount of content that is not retained. To grasp the chart's message, lay a straightedge along the line under the top section of the cone. Now imagine that the rectangle represents the material being presented using words only (say in a sermon). The space within the triangle represents the percentage of the material the hearer will retain. The rest will be lost. Now, slide the straightedge to sit along the line below section 3. Note how the percentage of what is retained has grown. As you ponder this difference, remember that studies underlying this chart were conducted as television was just beginning to change our culture to visual orientation rather than print and audio orientation. Current studies would probably suggest a cone that is much thinner at the top.

Because we retain more of what we both see and hear than of

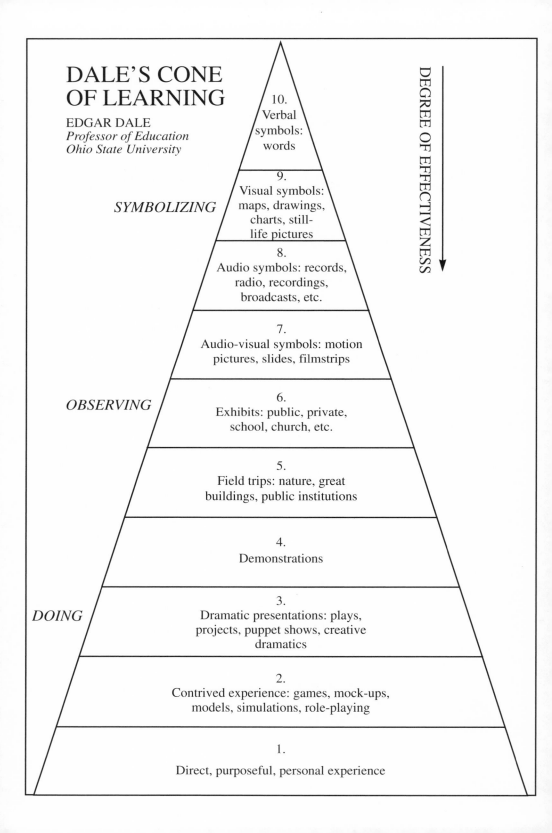

what we only hear, it makes sense for preachers who want their listeners to retain the content of their sermons to present that content visually as well as audibly. Adding a visual element accomplishes two tasks: first, it captures the attention of the children and thus helps them pay attention to the words spoken; and second, it makes at least one point of the sermon even more memorable than it would otherwise have been.

This is not a radical, new idea. The Gospels are filled with parables and teachings that Jesus attached to specific, everyday objects. Indeed, the Gospels preserve very few extended abstract teachings of Jesus. We are left to draw one of two conclusions. Either Jesus chose to tie most of his teachings to everyday objects or Jesus' abstract teachings were largely forgotten by his listeners who recorded what they remembered of what he said, that is, they remembered those teachings that were tied to concrete items. In either case, the learning for preachers is the same. A visual connection for sermons helps people of all ages pay attention and retain what is said.

In spite of Jesus' example, preaching has remained a predominantly auditory exercise. One can, however, add visual elements without going high-tech or becoming avant-garde. All that is required is to identify sermon props that are already in place in the sanctuary and to gather props related to the texts for the day and points of the sermon.

One warning: There is an important difference in using props as object lessons and using props to illustrate a sermon. In object lessons, the prop symbolizes the point. When recalling the object, the listener says "Oh, that is like . . ." Children are incapable of such thinking. However, a prop can be used simply to recall what the preacher said. In that case the listener says, "Oh, that reminds me of what the preacher said about . . ." Children appreciate and collect such reminders.

The Sermon Props All Around You

A sanctuary is as full of sermon props as Jesus' world was. The shape of the room, the way it is arranged, its furnishings, paraments (with their changing liturgical colors), banners, windows, paintings, sculptures, Christian symbols, the robes worship leaders wear—all of these things can be pointed out, explained, and woven into sermons.

The *Good News Bible* titled Joshua 4 "Memorial Stones Are Set Up." In so doing, it provides an interesting term and a challenge. Joshua 4 is the story of Joshua and the people of Israel crossing the Jordan River to enter the promised land. Following God's instructions, Joshua and the leaders carry large stones across the river, then pile them on the bank. After the crossing, Joshua explains that the stones are to be left there so that when children pass them, they, with their natural curiosity, will ask their parents, "What are the stones for?" thus giving parents an opening to retell the story of coming out of Egypt and into the promised land. The stones are reminders, or, to paraphrase the *Good News Bible,* "memory stones."

Joshua does not go into detail on the preservation of memory stones, but one thing is fairly obvious. Memory stones are only useful if there are people around who know the story the stones enshrine and can tell those stories when the questions are asked. Without the storytellers, the pile of stones is dismantled when the stones are needed for other things or the stones become insignificant shrines that are preserved but never understood.

Most churches have memory stones—or potential memory stones. Part of the preacher's task is to keep the story behind the stones alive, to be sure that members of the congregation can tell the story when questions are asked and to preserve the power of the stones to carry the true story of the community's past and to shape its present and future.

An elder in one church I served introduced me to a "memory stone" for that congregation. It was a gravestone. The grave was that of a much-loved and respected African American Christian who had been a slave of a member of the Caucasian congregation. Every Sunday he had stayed outside beside the horse and buggy. When he became a free man, he requested membership in the church. The church struggled, but voted to receive him. When he died, his last wish was to be buried in the church cemetery, a privilege of all members. The church struggled again. Finally they granted his wish, but sited his grave far away from the rest of the graves, right next to the tree ring where he had tied up the horses for so many years. At the time it was a very out-of-the-way spot. But years later when roads were being paved, the grave was right in the middle of the road. Today the road goes around the grave, making it the most noticed grave in the cemetery and providing the congregation with what could be a very significant memory stone. But the story has to be told and retold and interpreted in light of the "good news." Including it as a sermon illustration or telling it in order to connect a theological truth to everyday life definitely preaches.

Memory stones do not have to be unusual objects, unique to one congregation. Very common objects become memory stones when their stories are told and their functions are explained and tied to truths of the faith.

> Many congregations display lighted candles during worship. Some light candles at the beginning of worship and extinguish them at the close of worship with varying degrees of ceremony. Until worshipers know "why we do this," lighting candles is just something we do in worship. But when lighting the candles is explained in a sermon, three things happen: the flames become memory stones declaring God's presence with us in worship (or whatever meaning your congregation ascribes to candles), children hear the story from the congregation's leader, and adults are equipped to retell the story as children ask about it.

> Many congregations hang pictures of past preachers in the hallways of the building. When children can point out to one another the one who married Mama and Daddy, the preacher who was here when the church burned down, or the preacher who led the medical mission trip to Mexico, the pictures are memory stones. Those pictures can be carried one at a time into the sanctuary and displayed during a sermon illustrated with a story about that particular time in the congregation's history.

Using memory stones as sermon props does two things. It keeps the stories behind the stones alive and it adds a permanent, visual reminder of a sermon point. It is not uncommon for preachers to feature memory stones during children's sermons, for example, meeting children at the baptismal font during a service that includes a baptism. But it is also possible to build the stones into the "real" sermon.

In a sermon about Christian community, one preacher moved to the baptismal font to talk about how baptism brings us into the community, then returned to the pulpit. When he stepped out of the pulpit, worshipers of all ages looked up to see what he was doing. Hardly anyone missed what he said about baptism at the font, and most stayed with him for at least a while as he returned to the pulpit. He talked as he moved from one place to the other, making the baptismal font a very smooth, integral part of the sermon. Comments at baptisms in later months indicated that people heard and appreciated what the preacher had said.

HOMEWORK: LEAVE NO STONE UNTURNED

Go to the sanctuary. Sit in a pew. Look all around you. Make a list of all the memory stones in the room. What stories do they call to mind? When and how have they been used and how are they important in the life of the congregation? What truths do those stories call us to remember and live by? Pay attention to:
- The shape of the building
- Crosses and other Christian symbols in the room
- Special windows
- Furnishings: pulpit, altar/communion table, baptismal font, the organ, rugs
- Art work: banners, sculptures, paintings, paraments
- Items used regularly in worship: communion sets, Bibles, candlesticks, offering plates

Walk around the church and its grounds to identify all the memory stones.

- Paintings and photographs on the walls
- Different rooms: classrooms, kitchen, parlor, library, closets, and rest rooms
- Historic trees, gardens
- Memorial plaques, gravestones in the cemetery

Let the Flowers (As Well as the Stones) Speak Out

Many congregations display flowers in the chancel area during worship. Often they are simply there to add a beautiful touch of color and reminder of the natural world. But the flowers displayed can become part of the sermon.

A YEAR'S WORTH OF FLORAL DISPLAYS THAT PREACH

Advent wreath
    Preach about the candles lit that Sunday.
Chrismon and Jesse trees
    Refer during sermons to the meaning of specific ornaments.
Poinsettias
    Tell some of the legends about the plant.
Palm branches on Palm Sunday
    Explain how palm branches were used and their meaning in the streets of Jerusalem, then send branches home for display during Holy Week.
Easter lilies
    Explain why these flower-bearing bulbs have become Easter symbols.
Red flowers on Pentecost
    After preaching about the tongues of fire and the gift of the Spirit, give worshipers red flowers to wear, take home, or pass on to someone else as signs of the Spirit.
Baskets of bread from around the world on World Communion Sunday
Cornucopia (of fruit and/or canned goods) at Thanksgiving
Thorns to illustrate psalms and parables about weeds and thorns
    (Some very striking arrangements can be made of weeds and thorns!)
Grapes to illustrate texts that feature grapes and vineyards
A lush plant next to a dead branch to illustrate texts such as Psalm 1 or Jeremiah 17.
Pass out or tape onto bulletins a tiny seed of a large plant displayed in the chancel or of a large tree in the church yard.

The Bible is full of references to growing things. Many of these can appear in floral displays. For example, preaching on texts that feature vineyards comes to life when grapevines and clusters of grapes sit nearby. When the preacher can point to real grapes and grapevines rather than simply describe with words what they look like, children pay attention and the stories told are clearer.

Bring Your Own Props

Preaching texts are full of "stuff." It is one thing to talk about the stuff. It is another much more appealing and vivid thing to see and handle the stuff. Most pulpits even provide a ledge on which "stuff" can be easily displayed.

One of the most memorable sermons I have heard featured a baby bottle. Before the preacher read the scripture, Paul's letter to the church at Corinth, he produced the bottle and asked the congregation to listen for who Paul thought deserved a baby bottle for lunch. He set the bottle on the pulpit railing and read 1 Corinthians 3:1-4. There were knowing looks and grins exchanged among listeners. The preacher left the bottle in full view, picking it up occasionally during the sermon to offer it to different groups within the society that are acting immaturely. The children may not have understood every point in the sermon, but they did understand Paul's message that Christians are to grow beyond acting like babies.

When preaching on Jeremiah's leaky cisterns, another preacher perched on the pulpit rail two big glasses, one filled with clear water, the other filled with brown muddy water. He asked the congregation which they would rather drink, then read Jeremiah's indictment. Occasionally during the sermon, he picked up one of the glasses to contemplate and discuss. The symbolism spoke to children and to adults in different ways. For the children, it simply provided a visual stimulus to help them pay attention to and recall Jeremiah's prophecy. The adults thought about the water in a more abstract way AND reaped the same benefits as the children.

Basically, there are two kinds of props: those items that appear in the biblical text on which a sermon is based, and those that serve as a hook to capture attention for the sermon's topic. The baby bottle and glasses of water are examples of the former. They both appear in the text. Examples of props that may not appear in the day's text but which help make its point also abound.

Preaching on Christ the King or Palm Sunday is often clarified by the presence of two crowns, one a crown of thorns, the other a royal crown (perhaps from the Christmas pageant costumes). During the sermon on the kingship Jesus chose, the preacher can point out how it would feel to wear each crown, what it would be like to be a subject of the king who wore each one, and so forth. The crowns might replace flowers on the central table or could be displayed on a small table near the center of the chancel. The preacher might leave the pulpit to handle the crowns or simply point to them.

In addition, our lives are filled with items that capture theological truths for us and can capture the attention of children. One preacher in a large congregation introduced a sermon on sabbath keeping by showing the congregation a small statue that had been given to him by a friend. It was only eight inches tall, so he had to describe it for those of us near the back. It was a figure of a person in a striped T-shirt and tennis shoes. It was titled, "God on the Sabbath." The preacher talked about what the statue said to him and why he kept it where he could see it often. He promised to leave it on the pulpit after the sermon so people sitting near the back could come see it. Lots of children (and adults) stopped to look at it. Later when they saw the statue in his office, they felt closer to him because it was a personal item that they knew about.

No preacher will want to use props with every sermon. But . . .

when children see some *thing,* they often listen to words they might otherwise have ignored, simply to find out what the thing is and why it is there.

when a point can be illustrated with an object, displaying that object makes its point more memorable than describing the object does.

when a congregation's memory stones are mentioned and their stories told in preaching, the stone's power to shape the lives of both individuals or the congregation that sees them grows.

when children connect a story to a specific item, they recall the sermon every time they see that item.

8

Assigning Sermon Seat Work

Children are adept at and even more comfortable when doing several things at once. They grow up with radio, CD players, TV, computer games—often going all at once. They play computer games while watching TV and talking on the phone. Many successfully complete homework in front of the television—often to their parents' distress. And then they come to the sanctuary where they are expected to sit still and listen. There is much to be said for sitting quietly and listening in spite of, or perhaps especially in, our busy, active world. But it is an art that most people need to cultivate. We can no longer assume that it is an art children will master elsewhere. So if children are to learn to listen to sermons, we will need to offer them some help.

One way to help children listen is to provide them with activities to do with their hands while they are listening. We can invite them to draw pictures, solve paper and pencil puzzles, even look through a related storybook. These activities, when thoughtfully planned, are like training wheels on a bicycle. They provide support to the novice while he or she catches on—in this case while catching on to listening to a sermon. Initially, children will focus on the activities. Then slowly they will begin paying more attention to the sermon, "doing the activities in their heads" instead of with a pencil, and finally concentrating on the sermon and ignoring the activities entirely.

The question often raised about such activities is whether they are an encouragement to listen to the sermon or a distraction. It is an important question and one without a simple answer. For example, a mother reports that on Sunday her eight-year-old son looked up from his drawing of rocket ships during his father's pronouncement of the assurance of pardon—which was used in that congregation each Sunday—to whisper to no one in particular, "Smooth move, Dad. You left out 'reigns in glory.' " He was right. His mother was amazed. On the other hand, a twelve-year-old engrossed in a *Goosebumps* mystery never noticed when the sermon ended and the celebration of communion began. Drawing helped the first child listen. Reading the mystery distracted the second one. So what makes the difference?

The difference is that such activities hurt when they are totally unrelated to the sermon and are provided to keep children occupied so that the adults can listen in peace. The activities hurt when they (or the adults who distribute them) say to the children that the sermon is really not for them and that these activities are something for them to do instead of listening to the sermon. In short, the activities hurt when they discourage instead of encourage attention to the sermon.

On the other hand, the activities help when they (and the adults who distribute them) say to the children that listening to sermons is important and challenging work. The activities help when the children know they are offered to help them listen better. The activities help when they are designed to help children listen to particular sermons.

Oftentimes, there is a fine line between what helps and what hinders. A riveting book or computer game generally hinders. The reader is seldom aware of what is going on in the sanctuary. But leafing through a Bible storybook, especially one on the text for the day, often gives readers something to do, but keeps them alert enough to the world around them that they are available to tune in when they hear the name of the person or event they are reading about mentioned in the sermon. Doing a crossword puzzle on an unrelated topic does not encourage participation. But a crossword puzzle using key words in the sermon encourages children to pay attention when they hear those words. These activities hinder when parents give them to children and say, "Here is something to amuse you. Now be quiet so I and the other grown-ups can worship." But these activities help when a parent pays attention to what the child is doing and helps point out the connection to the sermon either in the sanctuary or in the car on the way home.

The trick is twofold. We must provide activities carefully designed to invite children to listen to the sermon. And we must teach parents and other adults in the sanctuary what the activities are for and how to help children use them. This latter task will be discussed in the next chapter. First we need to pay attention to finding existing activites or designing new activities. This is a fairly new science. At this point in its development, there are not many activities that have been proven to be successes or failures. Instead, preachers are experimenting with a number of possibilities.

Children's Bulletins and Worship Kits

A children's worship kit is a small bag or folder of materials designed to help young worshipers participate in worship. There are different kinds of kits for readers and nonreaders.

The *nonreaders' kit* is generally a small canvas bag with several pockets. One pocket is for the child's offering that is put in the plate when it is passed. Another pocket holds a small piece of hard candy that the child can enjoy as the sermon begins. In another pocket, there is a small picture book based on Bible stories or Christian themes. And the main compartment contains a small stuffed animal. One congregation provides a fold-out kit that becomes a stage of the sanctuary on which children can use included finger puppets representing worship leaders and worshipers. These bags offer the young child two things for the sermon: a piece of candy to be given to the child with the invitation to settle back and snuggle into a handy adult (young children respond to sermons as a total experience rather than by listening to any particular content); and something to do quietly (play with soft toys) during the sermon to keep active bodies occupied. Some congregations prepare and provide this bag each Sunday. Others give a bag to each child at baptism (or some other appropriate time) so that parents and children can pack their own unique bag each week.

The *readers' kit* includes bookmarks with which to locate hymns and Bible readings for the day, a pencil or several crayons, and sheets of paper. The paper may be small blank pads on which children are invited to draw pictures, Bible games or puzzles, or a child's form of the day's bulletin. Readers' worship kits are generally handed by ushers to children as they enter the sanctuary.

The heart of the readers' kit is the paper and pencil activity provided. What is provided can make a big difference in how well children are drawn into worship—especially the sermon.

The first worship aid especially for children in the Presbyterian Church was a small pad of paper titled, "For little Presbyterians" that were placed in pew racks. The expectation was that children would draw on the pad using the pew pencils. These led to paper and pencil Bible games "so that children would doodle on Christian themes." That was an improvement, but led to the wish that the games be matched to the texts and themes of the day. Some congregations began creating their "worship worksheets" by copying puzzles from books or creating their own to match the day's worship themes. Next, lectionary-based worship worksheets became available from several publishers. Although this seemed the perfect solution for those churches using the lectionary, two problems developed. First, as many people had already suspected, two preachers can create two very different worship experiences and sermons from the same texts. It was sometimes difficult for adults to identify the connection between what was on the worship worksheet and what was going on in their particular sanctuary. The second problem was that even when the sheet's contents did match the sermon and worship, the children often missed the connection. They simply enjoyed the puzzles without being drawn into worship through them. So worship worksheets evolved into children's bulletins, which put the order of worship into a child-friendly format and language. The pencil and paper activities are printed with the section of worship to which they are connected. So if children are instructed to decode words that are featured in the sermon, those coded words are placed in the printed order of worship alongside the sermon topic. (See sample in the appendix.) Response to children's bulletins indicates that they are not perfect either. They work well for children whose parents work with them diligently during worship (more on that in the next chapter). But by the time children have sufficient reading skills to use the bulletin independently, their need for and interest in the bulletin has already passed. More work and creativity is needed.

When children's worship worksheets or bulletins are created, it is important to include an activity that draws children into the sermon. These possibilities are endless.

1. Pose a task or question that alerts children to the outline of the sermon.

> Listen for three big questions Dr. Jones asks in the sermon. Write them below.
>
> 1. _____?
>
> 2. _____?
>
> 3. _____?

2. Invite children to illustrate something the preacher is going to describe.

> Draw a picture of the man who came to the big church in Dr. K's story at the beginning of the sermon.

3. Feature a word that will be used frequently in the sermon.

You will hear a lot about GRACE today. Circle three words below that go with GRACE. Cross out the three that do NOT go with grace. The sermon will help.

LOVE	**GRUDGE**	**ANGRY**
PATIENCE	**FORGIVE**	**JEALOUSY**

4. Offer puzzles based on key words and phrases.

Fill in the dotted  to find the word

Turn the letters of a W☺RD into pictures of the word.

Connect numbered dots to find the \\/\/ords

Add related words to each letter of the key word.

L o y a l

O b e y

f o r g i **V** e

E n e m i e s

Fit key words of the sermon into a crossword puzzle format. Provide a written clue for each word

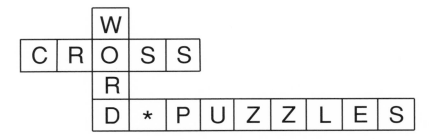

5. Challenge children to decode key words and phrases.

Substitute numbers for each

L	E	T	T	E	R
12	5	20	20	5	18

Write the phrase ƧᗡЯAWʞƆAꓭ

Addx aɋn extmra lɑetter tɀo eʞach wormd iƀn thʑe pʞhrase

Scramble the letters in each **WDRO**

Phrase the scramble in words the

Scramble the words in the phrase

Cross out **E~~Q~~V~~X~~E~~F~~R~~B~~Y** other letter

F_ill _in the_ m_i_ss_i_ng v_ow_els

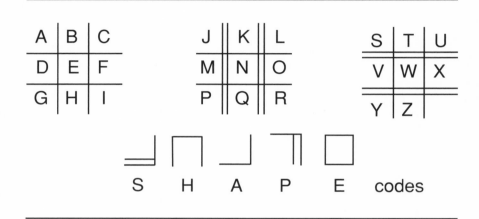

S H A P E codes

letters of a word
arranged like a brand

Write the next letter of the alphabet.

Z K O G Z A D S

A L P H A B E T

Telephone   2-3   6-3   3-1   3-2
              C   O   D   E

(Each letter is identified by the numbered button on which it appears and its place among the three letters on that number. For example, in the first number clue above, one would look at the second button and then locate the third letter on that button in order to discover the hidden letter "C.")

PI✪TUR★ ✪OD★S

✪=C   ★=E

Encouraging Sermon Art

Producing weekly children's bulletins with activities designed to draw children into the sermon requires volunteers or staff with the time, ability, and inclination to devote about two hours each week to the project. When that is not available, preachers can still encourage children to draw pictures or write ideas related to the sermon. The only requirement is that paper, pencils, or crayons be provided. A sample bulletin is provided in the appendix.

The first part of the preacher's task is then to suggest drawing and writing projects at the beginning of or at appropriate points within the sermon. For example:

> Before reading the scripture story text on which a sermon is based, invite the children to listen and draw a picture of what happened. Suggest that you will be exploring the story in the sermon and that they may get some ideas from the sermon about things to add to their picture or ways to draw their pictures.

> As you start a topical sermon, assign the children the task of drawing pictures of people demonstrating that quality or living out that principle, for example, "Today we are going to be thinking together about forgiving. It is not easy to forgive. While I talk, I challenge you to draw pictures of people showing forgiveness."

> When launching into a story in the middle of a sermon, say, "I think I know what it looked like when this happened, and I'd be curious to see pictures of what some of you think it looked like."

The second part of the preacher's task is equally important. The preacher needs to express interest in and respond to the children's creations. This can be done in many ways.

The simplest way is to hold brief conversations with children about their art as they leave the sanctuary with their parents. These need not be long discussions. For starters, simply asking to see a paper in a child's hand lets children know you are serious about their sermon art. At first, a shy child may simply show you the picture. All you need to do is comment about it ("Hey, that is a fine job!") or ask a question about a specific part of it (Point to a specific object and say "Tell me about that."). Once children sense your genuine interest in their work, they will generally show it off and tell you what it is about. You then have the opportunity of learning what in the sermon caught their attention and how they understood what you said. When they have picked up on what you intended for them, you can compliment them on their understanding. When they have taken your point a step further or put a new twist on it, you can say "Hmmm, I never thought of it that way!" or "You're right! I'll have to remember that this week." When they have drawn something seemingly off the topic of the sermon, you can respond to what is there. "Hmmm, I can see that this is important to you. It's important to me too." Or "That's a good idea for a sermon!" Occasionally, a child will use this as an opportunity to present a situation that needs pastoral attention. Respond to it as the cry for help that it is.

Children know their sermon art is taken seriously when it does not end up on the floor in the backseat of the car. Parents can post sermon art on the refrigerator door with a brief conversation about it and the sermon. Preachers can respond to children's art by placing a bulletin board near the sanctuary strictly for communications between children and the preacher. Children may post their own sermon art there. Preachers may post collections of art on the same topic with a sign naming the topic. Some preachers also leave messages for children on the board with suggestions for art in this morning's sermon or little love notes about things that children are concerned about this week: report cards, Halloween, or whatever. One preacher devotes the door of his office to this art.

Children's sermon art can also be saved and (with the artist's permission) used in a variety of ways. Copiers make it possible to shrink, enlarge, and reproduce children's art—even in color—at very reasonable prices! That means children's art can become bulletin covers, can be used as clip art in newsletters, and can be featured in special letterheads for stewardship and seasonal letters to the congregation. When enlarged, sermon art makes great posters announcing church events. It can also be filed to be displayed as sermon props in the future. The possibilities are almost endless.

More Than Drawings

Sermon art generally is drawings. But it can also include creative writing too. Some children quickly develop a preference for expressing themselves with words rather than pictures. Older children, especially, can

> listen for words to tie onto a key word or the name of key person.
> write their own definitions of a key word in the sermon.
> write diary entries for people who "were there" in the day's story.
> write their own prayer about. . . .
> write a prayer that the key person might have prayed.
> write the preacher a letter about. . . .

Their work deserves the same interest, conversation response, and use in the life of the congregation as do the pictures of the young artists.

Children's Corner

Smaller churches have another option. A corner of the sanctuary can be set up as a children's corner. A square of carpet can be laid on a tile floor in the corner and set up with a few stuffed animals for the younger children, and paper, crayons, and pencils for the older children. When the corner is near the front (probably on the side opposite the pulpit), children feel very much in the middle of things rather than pushed "out of the way" to the back. In one congregation that meets in a school, the preacher unrolls the carpet with some ceremony at the beginning of the sermon, invites the children to use it quietly, and speaks briefly to the children, often suggesting an art project tied to the sermon. Another preacher invites children to this corner and assigns a particular task to work on during the sermon. She often comes to the corner at some point in the sermon to talk with the children about what they are doing and knits that into the sermon.

Obviously children's corners work only in congregations that expect fewer than ten children on any given Sunday and that have a somewhat informal worship style. Even in these congregations care must be taken by both parents and preachers to help children realize when they are free to move to and fro between their families and the children's corner and when it is necessary to be quiet.

A New Term for the Congregation's Worship Vocabulary: Sermon Art

Simply using the term "sermon art" can create the expectation in the congregation that part of a sermon is the drawings and writings that children produce as they listen and respond to what they hear. This alerts the adults to the fact that children drawing or writing during the sermon is acceptable and actually a good way of learning to listen to sermons. And it suggests to children that sermons are for them, too. They may not understand everything that is said, but they can understand specific parts of it and know that they have a part to play in the congregation's proclamation of the Word. Finally, when the preacher becomes the curator of the children's sermon art, a special bond between the artists and the preacher is forged and the belonging faith of the children is richly nurtured.

9

Helping Parents Help Children Listen to Sermons

Some children become worship lovers early in life. I have known four-year-olds who choose the sanctuary over the nursery, and elementary schoolers who like worship and have an amazing grasp of what is going on. There are, of course, other children for whom time spent in the sanctuary is a trial. There is no undisputed theory about what makes the difference. Part of it seems to be something God creates in some children. But I have noticed that one thing most worship-loving children seem to share is an important adult who invites them to worship, communicates to the child that worship is important to them, expresses happiness in having the child as a worship partner, and is able to articulate some of the meaning of worship in a way the child understands. Most often this person is a parent, but it may also be a grandparent, other relative, or an adult in the congregation with whom a child forms a special attachment. (I will use the word "parent" in this chapter to refer to all these people fulfilling their baptismal promises to children by worshiping with them.)

One of the best gifts a preacher can give children is sermon-loving adults with whom to worship and begin listening to sermons. Unfortunately, the parents with whom many children come to the sanctuary are not sermon lovers, nor even skilled sermon listeners. Many are adults who desperately want good things for their children and sense that family participation in church is important. The majority are returning to the sanctuary after an absence that began in early adolescence and thus are themselves working with a child's understanding of worship and sermons. They need help. The good news is that many of them are ready, even eager, to get that help, if not for their own sakes, then for the sake of their children. They want to be able to understand what the preacher is saying and to be able to interpret it to their children.

So one way to preach to the kids is to teach and support their parents and to effectively equip them to introduce children to the fine art of listening to sermons. It is a task to which the church has not paid much attention. But it is not that difficult. Parents need two basic kinds of help. First, they need help clarifying their own understanding of worship in general and preaching in particular. And second, they need lots of very practical suggestions about how to help children learn to listen to sermons. The preacher who provides these things serves two generations at once.

Parents Need Help with the *Why* Questions

The first thing with which parents need help is clarifying and communicating their interest in worship. Over the last several years I have had the privilege of working through a simple two-question and one-task exercise with groups of parents. The first question is "When you go to worship on Sunday morning, what do you want, hope, expect for yourself?" If there is an honest parent in the group, the first answer is a groaning wish for "peace in the pew" or "just one hour of quiet." Everyone chuckles, acknowledges that reality, then begins digging out and clarifying the deeper reasons. It takes a while to sort through various understandings of the meaning and purpose of worship. When that conversation begins to reach conclusions, I pose the second question, "What do you want, hope, expect for your children when you bring them to worship?" It is usually not long before someone suggests that what we want for our children is the same thing we want for ourselves. After a little fine tuning of that realization, I remind folks of the question all parents eventually face on Sunday morning, "Do I hafta? Why?" and our tendency to pull a parental power play by saying something like, "Because I'm the parent and I said so. Now get your socks on!" More laughter. After these two questions, parents are then ready for the one task: in groups of four to six, create good answers to the question "Why do I hafta?" for a five-year-old, a seven-year-old, and a ten-year-old. When small groups share their ideas with the whole group, everyone is generally impressed with the possibilities. Participants often point to that as the first time they had ever attempted to articulate why they come to worship and become genuinely excited about being able to take up the conversation with their children.

These conversations deal with deep and important ideas about worship when the groups are composed only of nonclergy parents, however they get even more interesting when a pastor is around who adds in some of his or her hopes for and understandings of worship. These conversations tend to begin with worship and then focus in on sermons. They tend to begin with adult understanding and then progress to children's understanding. They are often identified as some of the few times sermon listeners and preachers have talked face-to-face about sermons. Preachers and listeners generally find the conversations beneficial.

This example suggests that preachers might initiate conversations with worshiping adults about the nature of worship and the purpose of the sermon. For some adults these conversations provide critical information that improves their ability to listen and respond to sermons. For other adults the conversations help get into words what worshipers understood at a gut level but have been unable to articulate for themselves or to their children. The result in either case is a good first step for both parents and children learning to listen to sermons.

Parents Need Help Talking with Children About Sermons

The Search Report (see chapter 1) found that children's faith development is enhanced when parents and children talk about faith together and when they worship together. This suggests that parent-child conversations about worship have great impact. Unfortunately, most parents are hesitant to initiate these conversations. Part of that hesitation comes from uncertainty about what to say and how to say it. So parents need both encouragement to initiate conversations and some conversation starters.

The encouragement is as simple as sharing the Search Report findings and pointing out to parents that they do more damage by being silent than by saying something inappropriate. (The latter can, after all, be straightened out in later conversations. The more conversations, the less likelihood of doing unfixable damage.)

Encouragement is also provided when preachers remind parents of their baptismal vows and point out that attending and discussing worship together is one good way to keep those promises.

Parents need to be urged to focus their conversations more on the content of worship and less on the child's behavior during worship. There are times when conversations about behavior (both complimentary and corrective) are essential. But when these are the only conversations about worship, children conclude that behavior is all that matters. To nourish interest in what is going on, children need conversations about the content of worship and sermons.

Parents need ideas about what they and their children might discuss. Some ideas may seem obvious, but parents need suggestions like the following:

- Recall and laugh at a joke or funny story the preacher told.
- Talk about how parent and child could work together to do what the preacher suggested.
- Parents tell children something they heard in the sermon and children tell what they heard.

- Share questions the sermon made you ask, then work on answering them together, or
- tell something you disagreed with and why you disagree with it.

Parents need to hear suggestions about good times for sermon discussions. One of the best times for this is in the car on the way home. Intentionally focusing on the good things that happened, for example, a favorite song, what the child learned, or a funny story, will keep the children involved in the conversation. Another reason to talk about the content of worship right after church is that the sermon is fresh in everyone's minds. Ideas can be reinforced before they get lost in the jumble of life. And of course, this may be the only time the family will be together and able to talk for the rest of the day, even for the next few days. Whether in the car, at lunch, or at bedtime, regular family conversations about the sermon encourage children to listen—just so they will have something to say.

Avoid negative comments as much as possible during this family time. For one thing, everyone is tired and hungry and ready to be on their own. So it is easy to be cranky and recall the morning's unpleasantries. When this is standard after-church conversation, children become worship critics and negative thoughts cast their shadows over the whole Sunday morning experience.

Preachers can help parents talk with their children even more by occasionally suggesting topics for conversation that can be discussed within each household. For example, during a Labor Day sermon about work, one preacher asked each household to make time that day to talk about the work that each member of the household does and then to pray together about each person's work. Parents, with fresh ideas about the importance of work from the sermon, were prepared to tell their children about their own work and to help the children identify and value the work they do in school and at home. Children heard their parents follow the preacher's suggestion by initiating the conversation (thus teaching them by example that sermons are meant to be acted on) and heard their parents' own ideas about the topics they had all heard explored in the sermon that morning (thus suggesting that sermons might be worth listening to).

Parents Need Practical Ideas About Helping Their Children Listen to Sermons

When parents have a child, they find that dinnertime is changed dramatically for the next eighteen years. Similarly, parents find that worship is changed. Parents can no more expect to worship in peace while their child worships in peace beside them than they can expect to eat in peace while their child eats beside them. Both worship and eating become something that is done *with* children. Eating with children involves providing nutritious food, helping children learn good table manners, sharing conversations that often lead to impromptu values-clarification exercises, and trying to build friendly relationships among family members. The process provides some awful experiences and some moments to treasure. Worshiping with children involves helping them participate in worship and sense God's presence; teaching them sanctuary manners; singing, praying, and listening with them; and trying to bond them to the church community. This process also provides some awful and some wonderful experiences. When this is pointed out to parents, they tend to laugh the laughter of recognition. Most have never thought of worshiping with children this way. Once they do, they set aside some unrealistic expectations and settle into the joys and traumas of the task at hand.

Just as there are some guidelines and tricks to eating with children, there are some guidelines and tricks to worshiping with children. On the next page there is a set of general guidelines for taking children to worship. Though these guidelines do not deal specifically with sermon listening, they help to set the stage for sermon listening. They look fairly simple and are probably common sense to experienced churchgoing parents. But we cannot assume that every parent with good intentions will automatically know these things. Printing them and discussing them in groups provides parents with essential tools for their work.

GUIDELINES FOR TAKING CHILDREN TO WORSHIP

1. Sunday morning starts on Saturday night.
   Lay out clothes, ready the offering envelopes, and gather together everything you'll need.
2. Make Sunday morning different!
   Set the alarm early enough to allow a relaxed pace.
   Have a simple, special Sunday breakfast.
3. As a rule, sit as a family and do not separate to sit with friends. (Friends tend to distract.)
4. Bring no distracting books, toys, or games to the sanctuary. (Refer to chapter 8, pp. 90-91.)
5. Plan ahead to avoid bathroom parades.
6. Worship WITH rather than BESIDE children.
   Stand children on the pew so that their ears, eyes, and mouths are near those of other worshipers as they sing, pray, and read together.
      Hum or la-la along with those who cannot yet read the words.
      Sing repeated phrases and choruses within hymns.
   Help young readers use hymnals and Bibles.
      Follow printed lines with a bookmark or the edge of the bulletin.
      Use the large-print hymnal. (Few children read music.)
   Whisper instructions.
      "Now is the time we tell God about stuff we are sorry about." "Listen to this story. It is a good one!"
   Whisper questions.
      "How do you think Jesus felt when that happened?"
      "What does this say about how you felt yesterday?"
   Whisper comments about what it means to you.
      After the doxology say, "My best blessing this week was our picnic!"
7. Avoid criticism and complaints fueled by fatigue and hunger in the car on the way home. Instead, hear what people did, enjoyed, and wondered about.
8. Enjoy holy hugs. There is much to be treasured and little to be embarrassed about when a twelve-year-old lays her head on her father's shoulder in church.
9. Be firm and consistent. Apply the same discipline for worship failures that is applied in other important matters.

Parents, as well as children, need to be introduced to any worship kits that are provided and taught how to use them. Using the nonreaders' kit is fairly easy. But using the readers' kit, especially with beginning readers, is a job best suited for a child with an adult partner. Parents need to set their bulletins aside and follow their children's. (For parents who are not very knowledgeable about worship, this is often a good learning experience.) Parents have to help children look up the hymns and readings and then help children keep up. Parents can help children with puzzles related to different parts of worship. This is especially helpful when the puzzles relate to the sermon. Parental help is necessary for children to grasp the points of contact between the puzzles and what the preacher is saying. One adult reports that from the time she could write, and continuing through her adolescence, she and her father wrote notes back and forth to each other on the margins of their bulletins. With his notes, her father kept her involved in what was going on and helped her make connections between what the preacher was saying and things that were going on in her life. Another parent has provided her older elementary school–aged daughters with worship journals in which to write during worship, especially during sermons.

A colleague who is also a parent shared two ways he helped his children learn to pay attention to sermons. He encouraged them to look for "take aways" and "windows."

> **"Take aways"** are ideas or stories that you really like and want to remember, to take away. The family often shares the "take aways" they found in the morning's sermon in the car on the way home. When several members of the family latched on to the same "take away," the family often referred to it in the following weeks. Occasionally, a take away would get printed or drawn and posted on the refrigerator door.
>
> **"Windows"** are things preachers say that make you think about something important that may or may not be what the preacher is talking about. When you find a window in a sermon, you crawl through it to think and pray about what is important to you. When you are through, you crawl back in and listen to the preacher again. Children can spot take aways before they spot windows. They need

to hear their parents describe windows that they themselves crawl through for a while before they catch on and spot windows of their own. (When they do catch on, children have learned an important thing about sermons: when listening to a sermon we listen less to what the preacher is saying and more to what God is saying to us through the preacher.)

Parents also need ideas for occupying a child during a sermon that has totally lost that particular child.

Look up and reread the day's scriptures. Draw or write about them. Think about what you would say about them if you were the preacher.

Read the words of the hymn that comes immediately after the sermon. Usually it is on the sermon subject. Practice reading it in order to be ready to sing it when the sermon is over. Pick a line or phrase to illustrate. Try to put it into your own words.

Reread all the printed prayers for the day. Underline the words that are used a lot. (Yes, "the," and "and" will get underlined, but so will some other words and it is a way to review the prayers.)

How?

It may sound as if parents need advanced theology, child psychology, and education degrees before they enter the sanctuary with their children. This is not true. What they need is a basic understanding of worship and a few helpful ideas. It is not very complicated and it offers parents a chance to grow in their own ability to worship and listen to sermons. The challenge is to find ways to get this information to parents. Again, that is not difficult. There are several possibilities.

Classes for parents about worshiping with children. Courses on parenting are often well received by parents. Four- to six-week courses that deal with a number of topics related to raising Christian children can be incorporated into the curriculum of

Sunday morning classes or offered on weeknights. Preachers and church educators can offer classes that meet on Sunday morning the option of a single Sunday class (possibly as a filler between two longer courses) on worshiping with children.

Classes can be offered for children and parents together. Since parents often need exactly the same basic information that children need in order to understand and participate in worship, they can benefit from learning together. Parents are especially open to this when they first bring their child to the sanctuary or when their child comes to the age at which he or she is expected to "stay for the sermon." Many denominations provide curriculum for one or two sessions on worship designed for parents and children to do together. The United Methodist Church offers curriculum that comes in a kit and can be used for group sessions or turned into learning centers set up at the church for parents and children to use together at their convenience.

Another parent and child course is still in the experimental stage. For a set number of weeks, parents and their children are invited to forgo their usual Sunday school classes to attend a class on worship as a family. During the class, families sit at separate tables and are led through exercises that help them prepare to go to that morning's worship and to reflect on it during the coming week. For example, the session that preceded a worship service about fear began with families writing and drawing on their paper-covered table things they are afraid of and telling one another stories about being afraid. They then looked up the key verse for the sermon, 1 John 4:18, and talked about what it says about relying on God when we are afraid. They also underlined all the fear words and the brave words in the call to worship, and explored a hymn about trusting God. By the end of the session they were well prepared to participate fully in that particular worship service and were curious to hear what the preacher would say. They also had some new ideas about how to pay attention to what is going in all worship services.

Many parents who will not attend a class will read a letter— especially if the letter is concise and arrives at a critical point. Letters that open with "your child is ready for a new experience . . .

and we want to share some ideas that will help you" are generally read and appreciated. Such letters are comprised of three short sections: first, they describe what the new situation is; second, they explain why it is important for your child; and third, they contain some very practical suggestions for making this new step go well for both parent and child. With the information in this book you can create such letters for

- children "graduating" from nursery care to worship attendance.

- children who have been leaving before the sermon for special activities but will now be expected to stay for the sermon.

- children who leave for choir during the school year but who will be expected to stay for the sermon during the summer.

In the appendix you will find a sample letter to parents of third graders who will begin staying in worship through the sermon.

There are endless possibilities to educate all the adults (not just the parents) by printing information in letters or short articles in the newsletter:

Articles explaining the use of worship kits alert nonparents to what children are doing with those pencils and paper and give the activities the church's blessing.

A letter that introduces a sermon series with a brief description of what is coming and suggests ways people of all ages can prepare for the sermons.

Short blurbs featuring one guideline from this book, a quote about preaching, or a comment from the preacher about listening to sermons are often more widely read and appreciated than full-page articles. (See sample newsletter "blurb" in the appendix.)

Parents are the members of the congregation who have the greatest impact on when and if their children learn to listen to sermons. If parents are to succeed at teaching their children the importance of listening to sermons, they need to realize that the job is theirs, have a sense of its importance, and be equipped with some guidelines and tools for doing their work. It is the congregation's task to equip parents for this work. Accomplishing this has dual benefits. The children are served and the parents grow as worshiping, sermon-hearing adults as they raise their children.

10

At the Back of the Church

After the sermon is preached and the last hymn sung, the preacher has one last chance to reach out to the children of the congregation. This chance comes as each child leaves the sanctuary. It is possible in the few moments available with each child to either redeem child-excluding situations in the sanctuary or to undo the good accomplished there. At its best this brief encounter is a reaffirmation of the child as a worshiper among God's people. Exactly what happens depends on the preacher, the child, and their relationship. It cannot be scripted in advance. There are, however, a few general guidelines.

As much as possible **meet the child physically on the child's level.** Lean over or stoop down to get to child-eye level. Shake hands, hug, give a high five, or offer whatever physical greeting you give other worshipers. Do not pat the head of any child not being carried in adult arms. (Children quickly realize that people pat the heads of babies and that being patted on the head somehow diminishes a person's importance.)

Greet the child by name. This requires real work in larger congregations! However, it is worth the effort because when you call a child by name you prove that he or she is known by you and is important to you, the leader of this church. You feed the child's belonging faith.

Do not say "My, aren't you cute today?" or "What a pretty dress!" or "My, aren't you growing?" Kids recognize those as phrases they hear from adults who do not know them as individuals or know what to say to them. They tend to feel devalued by such greetings unless they really do have on a special new dress or have gotten a haircut.

Instead say, "I'm glad you are here. I saw you singing . . ." or "I saw you praying" or "I liked singing . . . with you." to let them know that you value their presence as worshipers and that it is important to you that they are present and participating.

Do ask, "Did you do it?" when there was a sermon assignment or if the child is carrying a worship kit or piece of sermon art. If the answer is "yes," take a minute to inspect and comment on what the child has done. If the answer is "no," encourage the child to try the next one and promise to talk to him or her about it. Again, the goal is to let the child know that you care about him or her as a worshiper. The trick is to encourage participation without incurring guilt.

When it is needed, it is even possible to **say "I need your help."** If a school-age child is disrupting worship regularly, one way to resolve the situation is to ask the child to help you by changing his or her behavior. Tell the child what the problem is, describe how it affects you when you lead worship, and suggest a specific change that would really help you. When a preacher approaches a child about behavior that the child can, in fact, control, and if the child believes that the preacher likes him or her, the child will likely respond. When the preacher thanks the child the following Sunday, his or her sense of connection to the leader of the group is reinforced and the child's self-esteem is heightened. (A wink or grin at the parents generally lets them know that their child's behavior matters, but that they are not being judged by it. The preacher is willing and able to contribute to raising their child. Given this, parents generally try to help the child remember commitments made to the preacher.)

In short, just as the moment or two spent with the adults at the back of the church helps cement the bond between the preacher and the worshiper, the time spent with children also bonds both child and parents to the community of God's people, which the preacher represents.

11

A Final Word

This book does not offer a tight system of sequential steps to be taken in order to preach to children. It offers a grand collection of possibilities. There is no warning that if you leave out any one part, the whole effort will fail. You are not instructed to do everything mentioned. Instead, there is an invitation to try out the possibilities that make you say, "Hey, I could do that!" and to ignore the seemingly impossible possibilities (they are meant for someone else). So relax, experiment a little. Play with some new possibilities.

As you play, remember that the goal is not that every Sunday's sermon be one hundred percent child-friendly. Every sermon need not, indeed should not, be illustrated with stories from childhood, enhanced by visual props, accompanied by a children's sermon worksheet, and result in thoughtfully produced sermon art. Both children and adults would be overwhelmed! Instead, one sermon might bring to mind a scene from a childhood classic. Another sermon might call for a visual prop. And some very fine sermons will employ nothing tailored particularly for children. That's fine. Children are used to being with adults in situations beyond their total understanding and appreciation. They expect such experiences and even thrive on them when they sense that the events are important to the adults and that their participation is important to those adults. So your goal for the children should be: Give them enough direction and support so that their interest in and growing ability to listen to sermons is fed.

You are in charge. The fact that you are reading this book indicates that you care about preaching and about kids. You are probably already making efforts to preach to the kids. What you need is not a total overhaul of your preaching, but some fresh insights and some new possibilities to add to what you already do.

You can preach to the kids, too!

Appendix

BEWARE OF THE TRIP HOME!

By the time a family gets to the car at the end of Sunday morning, everyone is getting hungry, someone's shoes are pinching, most of us are ready to get out of church clothes, and nearly all are looking forward to some time on their own. In such situations it is easy to get in a downward spiral of negative comments and worship criticism. It is a good time to exercise the discipline of positive conversation. Make it a rule to talk only about the good stuff: the hymn you liked, the friend you saw, what you did in church school, the funny story the preacher told, and so forth. Ask children to save discussion of the mean name his big sister called him, how much she hated sitting by her brother, and how bored he was until everyone is safely home, fed, and in comfortable clothes. You'll be amazed how much easier it is to solve the problems later and how much better your whole family feels about worship when this discipline is observed.

Dear parents of a third grader:

Until now your child may have left the sanctuary before the sermon to attend children's chapel. Third graders, however, are ready to remain in the sanctuary for the entire service. Actually the next few years are prime time for them to be in the sanctuary learning our worship ways and being full participants in the congregation's worship—yes, even the sermon. It is an important way of putting down roots among God's people.

That does not mean that every Sunday will be a delightful experience. Listening to someone talk for fifteen minutes is not something children often do. Like learning to ride a bicycle, it takes time, requires lots of parental pushing, and generally involves some "skinned knees." It is also well worth the effort.

The following suggestions are offered to help you in this new endeavor:

● Pay attention to what you say to your child about worship in general and sermons in particular. Tell him why you want to go and why you want him to go. Express excitement that she is grown up enough to stay for the sermon. When the child complains about long sermons, respond with sympathy for the child's feelings but also with encouragement to keep listening. Your encouragement is critical.

● Sit together as a family rather than scattering to sit with friends. Friends distract. Children pay attention better and develop better worship skills by worshiping with their parents rather than with their friends.

● Remember that few children listen to entire sermons. Instead, they tune in and out as things catch their attention. The trick is to pay attention to what they do hear, not what they miss.

● Talk about sermons on the way home. (Make it a rule to talk more about worship content than about worship behavior.) Share things you heard that you enjoyed or learned from. Encourage your child to share what he hears. Listen together for "take aways," ideas or stories that you want to take away to remember.

● Instead of giving your child a book to read during the sermons (and thus suggesting that sermons are not worth her attention), write notes about the scripture and sermon to each other on the margins of the bulletin.

Children are an important part of this congregation. Your child is welcome, especially at this big step toward fuller participation in worship. Please call if I or anyone else can do anything to help you make it a happy, enriching step.

Faithfully yours,

SAMPLE CHILDREN'S BULLETIN

We Worship God Together on June 25, 1995

Shade in the spaces with a dot in them to find out what we are worshiping about today.

We Get Ready to Worship God

We listen to music and pray

We Light Candles of God's Presence

We Call Ourselves to Worship God Together

We call ourselves to worship

LEADER: God is our light and our salvation; whom shall we fear? God is the stronghold of our lives; of whom shall we be afraid?

PEOPLE: We will behold the beauty of God and make inquiry in God's house. We have come to worship and seek wisdom, to find shelter and help amid life's storms.

LEADER: God lifts us up from our doubts and fears, granting us confidence and courage.

PEOPLE: We will offer sacrifices of joy and thanksgiving. We will sing and make melody to our God.

We sing: Praise the Lord, praise the Lord,
Let the earth hear His voice!
Praise the Lord, praise the Lord,
Let the people rejoice!
O come to the Father through Jesus the Son,
And give Him the glory; great things He hath done!

Dr. Kennedy gives us some reminders for the week

Mrs. Cox gives a report on her trip

We sign the friendship pad

Page 1

We Praise God

We praise God with a prayer

We sing Hymn 482   *"Praise Ye the Lord, the Almighty"*

ye ———— **hast** ———— **thy**

thou

When this hymn was written people used some different words. They said **thee** or **thou** or **ye** instead of you. They said **thy** instead of your. They said **hast** instead of have. Write above each of these words in verse 2 the words we would say today. Watch for other changed words as we sing the whole hymn.

thee

ye

Praise ye the Lord, who o'er all things so wondrously reigneth,

Shelters thee under His wings, yea so gently sustaineth!

Has thou not seen How thy desires e'er have been

Granted in what He ordaineth?

thou ———— **thy**

We Say We Are Sorry and Are Forgiven

We tell God we have sinned

Eternal God, we have embraced the wisdom of this world as if knowledge could save us and our own cleverness could protect us. Yet too often we are shaped by our fears, not by faith. We have said and done things unworthy of our calling as your children. Our thoughts have been so dominated by the past and the future that we have failed to live fully in the present. Our lives are filled with discontent, worry, and self-protective pursuits. We have not dared to follow Jesus, who turned the other cheek and embraced the power of love. Forgive our misplaced loyalties and fear-filled priorities, as we seek to embrace a new faithfulness.

We promise to try to do better by singing:

There is a place of quiet rest, Near to the heart of God.
A place where sin cannot molest, Near to the heart of God.
O Jesus, blest Redeemer, Sent from the heart of God,
Hold us, who wait before Thee, Near to the heart of God.

We remember that God forgives us

We sing, "Glory be to the Father . . ."

We Hear and Think About God's Word

We listen to God's Word in 1 John 4 (Selections)
Pew Bible, page 240

(Selections) means that Dr. Kennedy will read only the verses he selects from 1 John 4. The most important verse he will choose is 1 John 4:18. Unscramble the letters in each word below. Then listen for those words as Dr. Kennedy reads.

REETH SI ON ERFA NI OVEL.

—— ———— —— —— ———— —— ————.

TCEFREP ELVO SACTS TOU FARE.

——————— ———— ——— —— ——— ————.

We sing our thanks for God's Word in the Bible

Break Thou the Bread of Life, Dear Lord, to me,
As Thou didst break the loaves beside the sea.
Beyond the sacred page I seek Thee, Lord.
My spirit pants for thee, O living Word!

We listen to the choir sing God's Word

We think about God's Word with Dr. Kennedy

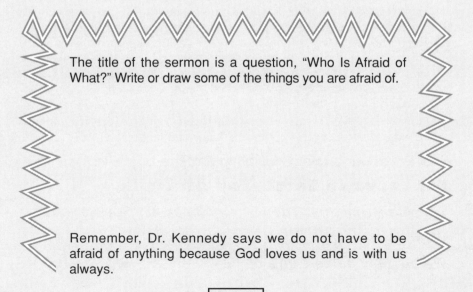

The title of the sermon is a question, "Who Is Afraid of What?" Write or draw some of the things you are afraid of.

Remember, Dr. Kennedy says we do not have to be afraid of anything because God loves us and is with us always.

We Say the Apostles' Creed

(It is on page 14 in the hymnbook.)

🎵 *We sing Hymn 345 "Dear Lord and Father of Mankind"*

We sing the Doxology
        —Praise God from whom all blessings flow . . .

We Respond to God's Word

We bring our gifts to God with this prayer

> We have rendered to Caesar much that we do not care to give, O God. Now we return to you the gifts that are yours. All our wealth and possessions belong to you. Bless our use of these resources, both what we bring for the church's ministry and outreach and what we keep to support ourselves and provide for those we love most. Amen.

We get ready to pray

> Spirit of the living God, fall afresh on me.
> Melt me, mold me, fill me, use me.

We pray together

 Write your own prayer about your fears.

Pray your prayer and join in on "The Lord's Prayer"

We Leave to Serve God All Week

🎵 *We sing Hymn 298 "There's a Wideness in God's Mercy"*

We follow the light of God into the world

We are sent out in God's name